The

701

Toughest

MOVIE TRIVIA QUESTIONS

of All Time

William MacAdams and Paul Nelson

A CITADEL PRESS BOOK
Published by Carol Publishing Group

A Citadel Press Book
Published by Carol Publishing Group
Citadel Press is a registered trademark of Carol Communications, Inc.
Editorial Offices: 600 Madison Avenue, New York, N.Y. 10022
Sales & Distribution Offices: 120 Enterprise Avenue, Secaucus, N.J. 07094
In Canada: Canadian Manda Group, One Atlantic Avenue, Suite 105, Toronto, Ontario M6K 3E7
Queries regarding rights and permissions should be addressed to
  Carol Publishing Group, 600 Madison Avenue, New York, N.Y. 10022

Carol Publishing Group books are available at special discounts for bulk purchases, sales promotion, fund-raising, or educational purposes. Special editions can be created to specifications.
For details, contact: Special Sales Department, Carol Publishing Group, 120 Enterprise Avenue, Secaucus, N.J. 07094

Manufactured in the United States of America
10 9 8 7 6 5 4 3 2 1

Library of Congress Cataloging-in-Publication Data

MacAdams, William.
  The 701 toughest movie trivia questions of all time / William MacAdams and Paul Nelson.
      p.   cm.
  "A Citadel Press book."
  ISBN 0–8065–1700–X   (pbk.)
  1. Motion pictures—Miscellanea.   I. Nelson, Paul, 1938–
II. Title.
PN1993.85.M25   1995
791.43—dc20   95-19763
                                                    CIP

For *Ephraim Katz,*
film encyclopedist without equal,
sorely missed

Also for Doris Ashbrook, Marc Furstenberg, Masami Mizuguchi, Mark Barr, Rob Slan, Dennis Block, Allan Richards, Warren Leming, and Bob Statzer, ascendant archaeologist of the cinema.

Thanks as well to James Agee, Don Allen, Joseph Anderson, Roy Armes, Charles Barr, André Bazin, Robert Benayoun, Maurice Bessy, Peter Bogdanovich, Patricia Bosworth, John Brady, Kevin Brownlow, *Cahiers du cinéma,* Ian and Elizabeth Cameron, Ernest Burns, Al Clark, Jay Cocks, Lester Cole, Jean Collet, Richard Combs, Jean-Pierre Coursodon, Peter Cowie, James Curtis, Jacques Doniol-Valcroze, William K. Everson, Manny Farber, *Film Comment,* Charles Flynn, Phillip French, Nicholas Garnham, José Luis Guarner, Leslie Halliwell, Forsyth Hardy, Phil Hardy, Ben Hecht, Charles Higham, Foster Hirsch, Diane Jacobs, Paul M. Jensen, Pauline Kael, Jim Kitses, Ado Kyrou, Pierre Leprohon, Phil Lyman of the Gotham Book Mart, Colin MacArthur, Joseph McBride, Todd McCarthy, Dwight Macdonald, Don Miller, Tom Milne, Jean Mitry, *Movie,* Rui Nogueira, William S. Pechter, Graham Petrie, *Positif,* Gerald Pratley, Michael Pye, Donald Richie, David Robinson, Jonathan Rosenbaum, Richard Roud, Martin Rubin, Georges Sadoul, Charles Thomas Samuels, Andrew Sarris, Pierre Sauvage, Steven Scheuer, Martin Scorsese, Paul Seydor, *Sight & Sound,* Alain Silver, Garner Simmons, Andrew Sinclair, Richard Stoddard, Jon Tuska, Kenneth Tynan, *Variety,* Elizabeth Ward, Robert Warshow, and Robin Wood.

Preface

The 701 Toughest Movie Trivia Questions of All Time is a book tailor-made to delight those of us who take our pleasures seriously—in this case, the joys of great cinema.

The book's eight quizzes pose questions about great films as well as historically important ones, films that critics, cinema scholars, and filmmakers alike consider exalting, transcendent, or merely situated on the "far side of Paradise" (as Andrew Sarris categorized the cinema's near great). *The 701 Toughest Movie Trivia Questions of All Time* is equally about the directors, screenwriters and cinematographers who crafted these films, and the actors and actresses who played in them. All eight quizzes are rated by stars: a one-star quiz is tough, a two-star quiz will tax confirmed movie buffs, and a three-star quiz will be a challenge for even the most knowledgeable cinéastes. The quizzes are subdivided into segments that include memorable lines of dialogue, first lines, last lines, characters' dying words, ad lines, working titles, original choices for roles, commonalities, lists of unheralded films, and quotes from critics, actors, and directors (often on other directors). There is also a photo quiz on the thirty films international critics have voted the greatest films ever made.

We hope we've succeeded in asking interesting questions that catch the art and the fun of movies. We also hope the anecdotes and the insights into cinema history included herein will spur our readers to have a look at some great films they've never seen before—and perhaps have never even heard of.

—WILLIAM MACADAMS AND PAUL NELSON

The

701

Toughest

MOVIE TRIVIA QUESTIONS

of All Time

QUIZ ONE

M E M O R A B L E   L I N E S

Name the films in which the following lines appear as well as the actors who spoke them:

■ **1.** " 'I think it would be fun to run a newspaper.' "

■ **2.** "Of all the gin joints in all the towns in all the world, she walks into mine."

■ **3.** ACTOR: "What are you thinking?"

ACTRESS: "Of all the people who've been born and have died while the trees went on living."

ACTOR: "Their true name is *sequoia sempervivum*— always green, ever living."

ACTRESS: "I don't like them."

ACTOR: "Why?"

ACTRESS: "Knowing I have to die."

ACTOR: "Here's a cross section of one of the old trees that's been cut down."

ACTRESS: "Somewhere in here I was born. And there I died. It was only a moment for you. You took no notice."

3

■ **4.** "I love the smell of napalm in the morning . . . it smelled like victory."

■ **5.** "There's something about working the streets I like. It's the tramp in me, I suppose."

☆ ☆ ☆

■ **6.** In what famous American film is there a breakfast scene that spans nine years?

■ **7.** Match the men in Column A with the women to whom they are—or once were—married in Column B:

COLUMN A	COLUMN B
1 Carlo Ponti	**a** Vivien Merchant
2 Mickey Rooney	**b** Judy Garland
3 Vincente Minnelli	**c** Dyan Cannon
4 Harold Pinter	**d** Julie Andrews
5 Charles Laughton	**e** Norma Shearer
6 Federico Fellini	**f** Sophia Loren
7 Roberto Rossellini	**g** Vivien Leigh
8 Cary Grant	**h** Ava Gardner
9 Blake Edwards	**i** Giulietta Masina
10 Irving Thalberg	**j** Elsa Lanchester
11 Laurence Olivier	**k** Nancy Allen
12 Brian De Palma	**l** Ingrid Bergman

■ **8.** He was a director who was justly famous for his tracking shots. James Mason starred in two of his films and wrote this poem about him. Name him.

> *I think I know the reason why*
> *Producers tend to make him cry.*
> *Inevitably they demand,*
> *Some stationary set-ups, and*
> *A shot that does not call for tracks*

Is agony for poor dear Max,
Who, separated from his dolly,
Is wrapped in deepest melancholy.
Once, when they took away his crane,
I thought he'd never smile again.

■ **9.** Match the actor in Column A with the film he directed in Column B:

COLUMN A	**COLUMN B**
1 Paul Newman	**a** *Reds*
2 Marlon Brando	**b** *The Alamo*
3 Dennis Hopper	**c** *Henry V*
4 Charles Laughton	**d** *Play Misty for Me*
5 Laurence Olivier	**e** *Easy Rider*
6 Warren Beatty	**f** *One-Eyed Jacks*
7 Clint Eastwood	**g** *Rachel, Rachel*
8 Robert Montgomery	**h** *The Night of the Hunter*
9 John Wayne	**i** *Lady in the Lake*

■ **10.** In what film do Buster Keaton, H. B. Warner, Anna Q. Nilsson, and Gloria Swanson play bridge?

D I R E C T O R S O N F I L M

Identify the directors who made the following statements:

■ **11.** "People confuse what I do with mystery. I don't believe in mystifying an audience. I believe in giving them all the information and then making them sweat."

■ **12.** "When I was a child, I suffered from an almost complete lack of words. My education was very rigid. My father was a priest. As a result, I lived in a private world of my own dreams. I played with my puppet theater. I had very few contacts with reality or channels to it. I was afraid of my father, my mother, my elder brother—everything. Playing with this puppet theater and a projection device I had was my only means of self-expression. I had great difficulty with fiction and reality. As a small child, I mixed them so much that my family always said I was a liar. Even when I grew up, I felt blocked."

■ **13.** "The cinema is truth twenty-four times a second."

■ **14.** "I'm fascinated by all forms of spectacle: theater, circus, cinema itself. ... When I show the atmosphere of show business, I speak of myself, because my life is a show. I am a man wholly devoted to spectacles."

■ **15.** "The final freeze was an accident. I told Léaud to look into the camera. He did, but quickly turned his eyes away. Since I wanted that brief look he gave me the moment before he turned, I had no choice but to hold on it: hence the freeze."

☆ ☆ ☆

■ **16.** In 1952, Michael Powell went to Hollywood looking for financing for his and Emeric Pressburger's next production, a bio-pic of Richard Strauss. Columbia's Harry Cohn offered them *Lawrence of Arabia*, which they refused. "At the time, I couldn't see it as a film," Powell wrote "I was blinded by this search for music . . . and Emeric wasn't interested in *Lawrence of Arabia* at all." True or False?

■ **17.** Run by Herbert J. Yates, this studio specialized in hackneyed B movies for twenty years before it gradually phased out film in favor of television production in the late fifties. Though Yates occasionally produced a prestigious picture (John Ford's

The Quiet Man, for example), his studio's pictures consisted mainly of cheap Westerns that starred Roy Rogers, Gene Autry, Johnny Mack Brown, and Bob Steele. Novelist Nathanael West made his living as a scriptwriter in this studio as did Yates's wife and favorite leading lady, frozen-faced Vera Hruba Ralston, whom nobody could make a star. Name the studio.

■ 18. Match the films in Column A with the alternative titles foisted upon them by certain wags in Column B:

COLUMN A

1 Barbra Streisand's *Yentl*
2 Jacques Rivette's *Paris Belongs to Us*
3 King Vidor's *Duel in the Sun*
4 Francis Coppola's *One From the Heart*
5 W. S. Van Dyke's *I Take This Woman*
6 Warren Beatty's *Reds*
7 Clint Eastwood's *Sudden Impact*

COLUMN B

a *I Retake This Woman*
b *One From the Computer*
c *Marienbad Belongs to Us*
d *Dirty Harriet*
e *Tootsie on the Roof*
f *Lust in the Dust*
g *Commie Dearest*

■ 19. An extremely popular hard-boiled novelist once played his own detective in a movie. Name the author, the detective, and the film.

■ 20. Name the actor who made the following statement before accepting one of his most famous roles: "Carol, I can't play this part! I can't do it. I can't work in a sewer. I come from California! My throat! I'm so cold." Name the film as well.

P O S T E R   A D   L I N E S

Name the films being advertised:

■ **21.** "They're young . . . they're in love . . . and they kill people."

■ **22.** "He talks . . ."

■ **23.** "There are angels on the streets of Berlin."

■ **24.** "China. 1920. One Master. Four Wives."

■ **25.** "What do you get when you cross a hopelessly straight, starving actor with a dynamite red-sequined dress? You get America's hottest new actress."

QUIZ ONE
☆ ☆

M E M O R A B L E   L I N E S

Name the films in which the following lines appear as well as the actors who spoke them:

■ **26.** "Don't want no money, Ethan. No money, Marty. Just a roof over Ol' Moses's head and a rocking chair by the fire. My own rocking chair by the fire, Marty."

■ **27.** "Where is the little comrade's room?"

■ **28.** "If you will permit me to say so, sir, the subject is not an interesting one. The poor know all about poverty, and only the morbid rich would find the topic glamorous. ... You see, sir, rich people and theorists—who are usually rich people—think of poverty in the negative, as a lack of riches, as disease might be called the lack of health. But it isn't, sir. Poverty is not the lack of anything, but a positive plague, virulent in itself, contagious as cholera, with filth, criminality, vice, and despair as only a few of its symptoms. It is to be stayed away from, even for purposes of study. It is to be shunned."

9

■ **29.** "You know, sometimes when you're out in the night and you look up at the stars, you can almost feel the motion of the earth. It's like a little ball that's turning through the night with us hanging on to it."

■ **30.** "Jim, do you think the end of the world will come at nighttime?"

☆ ☆ ☆

■ **31.** What do the middle initials in David O. Selznick's and Louis B. Mayer's names have in common?

■ **32.** Match the men in Column A with the women in Column B to whom they are—or once were—married:

COLUMN A	COLUMN B
1 Dudley Moore	**a** Pier Angeli
2 Jack Lemmon	**b** Patricia Medina
3 Jean-Luc Godard	**c** Felicia Farr
4 Ronald Colman	**d** Tuesday Weld
5 Stewart Granger	**e** Maria Montez
6 Vic Damone	**f** Julie London
7 Rod Steiger	**g** Jean Simmons
8 Jack Webb	**h** Claire Bloom
9 Joseph Cotten	**i** Candice Bergen
10 Garson Kanin	**j** Benita Hume
11 Louis Malle	**k** Anna Karina
12 Jean-Pierre Aumont	**l** Ruth Gordon

■ **33.** What famous American literary critic wrote the following poem about writers who journeyed to Hollywood to write movies?

What shining phantom folds its wings before us?
What apparition, smiling yet remote?

Is this—so portly yet so lightly porous—
That old friend who went west and never wrote?

■ **34.** Match the actor or actress in Column A with the film that he or she directed in Column B:

COLUMN A	COLUMN B
1 Elaine May	**a** *The Hired Hand*
2 Peter Fonda	**b** *Charlie Bubbles*
3 Albert Finney	**c** *Hide in Plain Sight*
4 Jeanne Moreau	**d** *Vivre ensemble*
5 Anna Karina	**e** *The Ceremony*
6 Laurence Harvey	**f** *La Lumière*
7 Jack Lemmon	**g** *Kotch*
8 James Caan	**h** *A New Leaf*

■ **35.** Name the famous British actor who, on his way back to England from a secret mission in Lisbon, was killed by the Luftwaffe, who thought they were shooting down a plane in which Winston Churchill was a passenger.

Directors on Film

Identify the directors who made the following statements:

■ **36.** "The only thing I can bring to this illogical, irresponsible, and cruel world is my love."

■ **37.** "Build your film on white, on silence, and on stillness."

■ **38.** "I think there is one thread running through all my pictures: the fight against Destiny, or Fate, or whatever you want to call it."

39. "When a director creates a little gem from time to time ... he certainly has the right to make some run-of-the-mill pictures."

40. "He who leaps into the void owes no explanation to those who watch."

☆ ☆ ☆

41. After starring in only three films, this actor was nominated for a Best Actor Oscar two years in a row (losing both times) and never made another film. Name him.

42. Worried about decreasing audience attendance, the studio offered a cash reward to its employees for suggestions to boost the box office. Name the famous screenwriter who quipped, "Let's show the movies in the streets—and drive the people back into the theaters."

43. Why does Alan Smithee get screen credit for directing the following movies when there is no such person as Alan Smithee: *Death of a Gunfighter, Fade In, Stitches, Let's Get Harry, Morgan Stewart's Coming Home, Ghost Fever, The Shrimp on the Barbie, Solar Crisis,* and *Fatal Charm?*

44. When Al Capone first saw Howard Hawks's *Scarface,* he hated how Hawks had depicted him and threatened to have him killed. True or false?

45. Name the classic film to which Ingmar Bergman was referring when he said: "I think it's an extremely bad picture. It is badly acted. ... It is irritating. It lacks style. I can't understand its humor, its complete lack of sensuality. The hunt is good, though."

P O S T E R   A D   L I N E S

Name the films being advertised:

■ **46.** "Overnight she became a star. Over many nights she became a legend."

■ **47.** "He had to find her . . . he had to find her . . ."

■ **48.** "Television will never be the same."

■ **49.** "Don't pronounce it . . . SEE IT!"

■ **50.** "This, too, was Lincoln!"

QUIZ ONE

★ ★ ★

M E M O R A B L E   L I N E S

Name the films in which the following lines appear as well as the actors who spoke them:

■ **51.** "There was an old lady on Main Street last night picked up a shoe. And the shoe had a foot in it."

■ **52.** "I just kept going down and down there. It was like going down to the bottom of the world—to find my brother. I found my brother's body there where they had thrown it away on the rocks by the river like an old dirty rag nobody wants. He was dead, and I felt I had killed him. . . . If a man's life can be lived so long and come out this way, like rubbish, then something was horrible and had to be ended one way or another, and I decided to help."

■ **53.** "Ever hear the one about the guy with the rash on his arm? Goes to a skin doctor. They try everything—creams, oils, injections—no go. Finally, he goes to a specialist in Copenhagen. The doctor asks him, 'What do you do for a living?' The guy says, 'I work in a circus. I give enemas to elephants. The thing is, to give an enema to an elephant, you have

to shove your arm up its ass.' The doctor says,
'That's it! You give up your job, and I guarantee
you the rash will go away.' The guy says, 'What?
Give up show business?' "

■ **54.** "I've seen things you people wouldn't believe At
tack ships on fire off the shoulder of Orion. I
watched sea beams glitter in the dark near the
Tannhauser Gate. All those moments will be lost in
time, like tears in rain. Time to die."

■ **55.** "I shoot first. It's my only defense against Fate."

☆ ☆ ☆

■ **56.** Clyde Bruckman's directorial career was ruined
when he was sued for "borrowing" scenes from comedian Harold Lloyd's movies for his own productions. Bruckman later committed suicide—in the
men's room of a restaurant where he'd just finished
a meal he couldn't pay for—with a pistol borrowed
from yet another famous comedian. Name him.

■ **57.** Match the men in Column A with the women
to whom they are—or once were—married in
Column B:

COLUMN A	**COLUMN B**
1 Anthony Mann	**a** Jeanne Moreau
2 William Holden	**b** Jean Simmons
3 Don Siegel	**c** Sarita Montiel
4 Richard Brooks	**d** Viveca Lindfors
5 Rudy Vallee	**e** Brenda Marshall
6 William Friedkin	**f** Anouk Aimée
7 Jean-Pierre Aumont	**g** Jane Greer
8 Jed Harris	**h** Anne Wiazemsky
9 Sean Connery	**i** Marisa Pavan

10 Jean-Luc Godard   **j** Diane Cilento
11 Albert Finney   **k** Ruth Gordon

■ **58.** Name the famous screenwriter who ended his
risqué poem, "Prayer to His Bosses," with these
lines:

> *Before I die or go berserk*
> *Oh let me write once Not To Fit*
> *Some big box office movie jerk*
> *Some million dollar piece of tit.*
> *Oh let my battered talents work*
> *On something besides baby shit.*

> *Oh let me grow one leaf of grass,*
> *One breath of truth, one cry of man's*
> *Travail and quest, one peal of brass*
> *To drive Art from its crapping cans—*
> *One tale that doesn't kiss the ass*
> *Of ninety million movie fans.*

■ **59.** Name the actor or actress in Column A with the
film that he or she directed in Column B:

COLUMN A	COLUMN B
1 Mickey Rooney	**a** *Posse*
2 Dick Powell	**b** *Split Second*
3 Ralph Richardson	**c** *The Kentuckian*
4 Walter Matthau	**d** *The Buccaneer*
5 Burt Lancaster	**e** *Remodeling Her Husband*
6 Frank Sinatra	**f** *My True Story*
7 Kirk Douglas	**g** *Gangster Story*
8 Toshiro Mifune	**h** *None But the Brave*
9 Lillian Gish	**i** *Home at Seven*
10 Anthony Quinn	**j** *The Legacy of the Five Hundred Thousand*

■ **60.** "I got one. I'm not sure about the other. ... I'm sorry. But it's all right now, baby. Come on, we've got to hurry." These were the last lines spoken by this erstwhile actor in his last film, just before he's shot dead by Lee Marvin. He said them to Angie Dickinson. The year was 1964. Name the actor and the film.

D I R E C T O R S   O N   F I L M

Identify the directors who made the following statements:

■ **61.** "In my whole life, I have never understood a single symbol."

■ **62.** "Cinema remains a machine, a light, and a white sheet."

■ **63.** "Shakespeare also cuts at strange times. His cutting is like a door through which the poetry enters."

■ **64.** "The only thing which never let me down in Hollywood was my camera."

■ **65.** "All the good things in this film were made by me. The things that are no good in it were made by others."

☆ ☆ ☆

■ **66.** Who coined the term *film noir*? Name the paperback series of hard-boiled crime novels published in France, bound in distinctive black covers, as well as the influential American magazines that put the *noir* in these films.

■ **67.** Name the American director who, during his days as a newspaper reporter, found the body of actress Jeanne Eagels, dead from an overdose of heroin.

■ **68.** Which of the following directors have won Oscars for Best Director? For what films?

a Buster Keaton	**h** Stanley Kubrick
b Howard Hawks	**i** Orson Welles
c Sam Peckinpah	**j** Alfred Hitchcock
d Otto Preminger	**k** Douglas Sirk
e Fritz Lang	**l** Harold Lloyd
f Ernst Lubitsch	**m** Josef von Sternberg
g D. W. Griffith	

■ **69.** In the midst of making a drama that would become a classic, this director—well-known for his comedies—was asked by his cinematographer how to shoot a monkey's funeral. "We'll use the standard monkey-funeral set-up," he quipped. Name the director and the film.

■ **70.** This moody, almost forgotten, low-budget movie was produced in 1943 by a man who knew Alfred Hitchcock and whose movies Hitchcock understandably admired. There is a scene in the picture that almost certainly inspired the murder of the character played by Janet Leigh while taking a shower in Hitchcock's *Psycho*, made seventeen years later. Name the film and its producer.

P O S T E R   A D   L I N E S

Name the films being advertised:

■ **71.** "A powerful story of 9 strange people."

■ **72.** "$2,000,000 payoff? Blood-splattered apartment and four dead bodies greeted the police at the 47th Precinct last night. Mass murder took place at 21 Walker Drive . . ."

■ **73.** "They have a date with fate in . . ."

■ **74.** "He doesn't break murder cases. He smashes them."

■ **75.** "She had the biggest Six-Shooters in the West!!!"

QUIZ TWO

Name the films in which the following lines appear as well as the actors who spoke them:

■ **76.** "I *am* big. It's the *pictures* that got small."

■ **77.** "The Atlantic Ocean was something then. Yes, you should have seen the Atlantic Ocean in those days."

■ **78.** "Say, answer me this one, will you? Why is gold worth some twenty bucks an ounce? ... A thousand men, say, go searching for gold. After six months, one of 'em's lucky. One out of a thousand. His find represents not only his own labor but that of nine hundred and ninety-nine others to boot. That's six thousand months or five hundred years scrabbling over a mountain, going hungry and thirsty. An ounce of gold, mister, is worth what it is because of the human labor that went into the finding and the getting of it. . . Well, there's no other explanation, mister. Gold in itself ain't good for nothing except for making jewelry with and gold teeth."

■ **79.** "Tell me, what do you do besides lure men to their doom on the Twentieth Century Limited?"

■ **80.** "This is my hand. I can move it, feel the blood pulsing through it. The sun is still high in the sky, and I, Antonius Block, am playing chess with Death."

☆ ☆ ☆

■ **81.** Name the movie, generally considered the first modern gangster film because its heroes were criminals, about which scriptwriter Ben Hecht said: "It was the first gangster film to bedazzle the movie fans; there were no lies in it—except for a half-dozen sentimental touches introduced by the director. I still shudder remembering one of them. My head villain, after robbing a bank, emerged with a suitcase full of money and paused in the crowded street to notice a blind beggar and give him a coin—before making his getaway."

■ **82.** As a child, he appeared in several silent films with his father, who was a famous actor. His sister was a leading lady in B Westerns during the forties. Primarily a low-budget cowboy star himself, he occasionally landed great roles with major directors, particularly Orson Welles and John Huston, but he also worked with Frank Borzage (*History Is Made at Night*) and John Ford (*Stagecoach, My Darling Clementine*). Name the actor.

■ **83.** Match the directors in Column A and the scriptwriters with whom they worked in Column B:

COLUMN A	COLUMN B
1 John Ford	**a** Graham Greene
2 Howard Hawks	**b** Harold Pinter

3 Vittorio De Sica   **c** Jacques Prévert
4 Billy Wilder   **d** Robert Bolt
5 Carol Reed   **e** Budd Schulberg
6 David Lean   **f** Alain Robbe-Grillet
7 Elia Kazan   **g** I. A. L. Diamond
8 Marcel Carné   **h** Frank S. Nugent
9 Alain Resnais   **i** Cesare Zavattini
10 Joseph Losey   **j** William Faulkner

■ **84.** Max and Dave Fleischer were Walt Disney's main rivals as animators in the thirties. Their most famous cartoon creation was killed in 1935 by the Hays Office. Name her.

■ **85.** This film's main characters are a big-time Broadway columnist, his confused younger sister, a sleazy press agent, and a naive jazz guitarist. No one in the film gets killed or even fires a gun or wields a knife. Only one person is beaten up. Yet this is one of the darkest, most violent *noir* films ever made, and the overall psychological destruction is certainly criminal. Name it.

■ **86.** Match the actors or actresses in Column A with the original choices for the roles in Column B:

COLUMN A

1 Oskar Werner in François Truffaut's *Fahrenheit 451*
2 Humphrey Bogart in Michael Curtiz's *Casablanca*
3 Isabelle Huppert in Joseph Losey's *The Trout*
4 Kirk Douglas in Elia Kazan's *The Arrangement*

COLUMN B

a Laurence Olivier

b Montgomery Clift

c Ava Gardner

d Jean-Paul Belmondo

5 James Dean in Elia Kazan's *East of Eden*

6 James Mason in George Cukor's *A Star Is Born*

7 Doris Day in Charles Vidor's *Love Me or Leave Me*

8 Alida Valli in Luchino Visconti's *Senso*

e Ronald Reagan

f Marlon Brando

g Ingrid Bergman

h Brigitte Bardot

■ **87.** "Actors!" he said. "I hate the sight of them! Actors are cattle—actresses, too. I tell them I hate the sight of them and they love it, the exhibitionists! Any profession that calls for a man to have to use paint and powder on his face in order to earn a living gives me evil thoughts. Think of it: little bits of powder, little bits of paint on the face of adult men and women so they can pay the rent. My own daughter Patricia made her Broadway debut recently. I sometimes shudder when I think of a daughter of mine doing that!" Name the director who had to live with these words.

■ **88.** Match the films in Column A (all remakes) with those in Column B (the original versions):

COLUMN A

1 Howard Hawks's *His Girl Friday*

2 John Ford's *Mogambo*

3 Bob Fosse's *Cabaret*

4 Warren Beatty's and Buck Henry's *Heaven Can Wait*

COLUMN B

a Alexander Hall's *Here Comes Mr. Jordan*

b Max Ophuls's *La Ronde*

c Leo McCarey's *Ruggles of Red Gap*

d Victor Fleming's *The Wizard of Oz*

5 Charles Walters's *High Society*

6 Roger Vadim's *Circle of Love*

7 Sidney Lumet's *The Wiz*

8 William Friedkin's *Sorcerer*

9 Bob Fosse's *Sweet Charity*

10 George Marshall's *Fancy Pants*

e Lewis Milestone's *The Front Page*

f Federico Fellini's *Nights of Cabiria*

g Victor Fleming's *Red Dust*

h Henry Cornelius's *I Am a Camera*

i H. G. Clouzot's *The Wages of Fear*

j George Cukor's *The Philadelphia Story*

■ **89.** By the early thirties, less than a decade after its inception, this studio had become the largest and most prestigious in Hollywood. In the forties, its slogan was "More stars than there are in the heavens." In the early seventies, after years of hard times, the studio peddled its own past by selling thousands of costumes and props to an auctioneer for $1.5 million. The auctioneer made a profit of $12 million (Judy Garland's red slippers from *The Wizard of Oz* went for $15,000). Name the studio.

■ **90.** A Rhodes scholar and an English instructor at West Point, this actor first gained acclaim as a singer-songwriter. In an infamous, underrated 1980 Western, he played an Oxford graduate who became a Wyoming sheriff. Name the actor and the film.

P O S T E R   A D   L I N E S

Name the films being advertised:

■ **91.** "Unchanged men in a changing land. Out of step, out of place and desperately out of time."

■ **92.** "He was new on the block, the pretty girl belonged to the leader of the gang and the leader of the gang called him 'chicken' to his face . . ."

■ **93.** "Marilyn Monroe and her bosom companions."

■ **94.** "It explodes in the no-man's land no picture ever dared cross before! Now the screen blasts open the bombshell story of a Colonel who led his regiment into hell and back while their maddened General waited for them—with a firing squad!"

■ **95.** "A beautiful coastline   a rich man wants to develop it. A poor beach bum wants to live on it. An entire town wants to profit by it. And a real-life mermaid wants to save it. . . . Only one of them will get their way."

■ **96.** "He has a yen for her, but he won't tell her where it's hidden."

■ **97.** "An Unforgettable Drama of a Japanese Soldier's Quest for Redemption in the Shocking Aftermath of War."

■ **98.** "An Uproarious Comedy About a Quartet of Bumbling Thieves who Attempt the Biggest Heist of their Lives." ·

■ **99.** "There's no speed limit and no brakes when Sullivan travels with Veronica Lake!"

■ **100.** "The land of the free gone wild! The heyday of the hotcha! The shock-crammed days G-men took ten years to lick!"

Quiz Two
★ ☆

M E M O R A B L E   L I N E S

Name the films in which the following lines appear as well as the actors who spoke them:

■ **101.** "I was born when you kissed me. I died when you left me. I lived a few days while you loved me."

■ **102.** "Out! I close the iron door on you."

■ **103.** "I can't help associating your lack of firmness with the decline of your family. Decrepit families imply deficient willpower and decadent conduct I thought you were a child of nature, but you were the last in a line of degenerate aristocrats."

■ **104.** "Listen, mister, when I come in here tonight, you seen an old clock running down. I'm tired. I'm through. Happens to everybody sometime. It'll happen to you, too, someday. With me, it's a little bit of everything. My back aches and head aches. I can't sleep nights. It's so hard to get up in the morning and get dressed and walk the streets, climb the stairs. I go right on doing it. Well, what am I gonna do, knock it? I have to go on making a living so I can die. But even a fancy funeral ain't worth waiting for if I've got to do business with crumbs like you. . . . So I don't get to have a fancy funeral after all. Anyway, I tried. Look, mister, I'm so tired you'd be doing me a big favor if you'd blow my head off."

■ **105.** "Someday a real rain'll come and wash all this scum off the streets."

☆ ☆ ☆

■ **106.** Though he made less than a dozen films, his career was not without distinction. In his first film (playing opposite Bette Davis), he was nominated for best Supporting Actor. One of his last movies was Stanley Kubrick's *Spartacus*. He's best remembered, however, for his performance in two classic crime films, one directed by Joseph H. Lewis and the other by Alfred Hitchcock. Said Lewis: "For the character of Bart, I wanted an actor who, by osmosis or scent or whatever, projected an inner weakness. I decided to cast a gay in the part. I didn't have to tell him how to play Bart or that I wanted him to express Bart's weakness. I knew he'd betray *himself*. Subtly and gently." Though Lewis's attitude toward homosexuals is certainly strange (since the film under discussion is memorable as a *heterosexual* love story), he got a performance that's as moving today as it was in 1949. Name the actor and the Lewis and Hitchcock films.

■ **107.** The *Louise* was the first British ship sunk by the Germans in World War I. In what film is a German gunboat named the *Louisa* sunk?

■ **108.** Match the directors in Column A and the scriptwriters with whom they often worked in Column B:

COLUMN A	COLUMN B
1 Budd Boetticher	**a** Theda von Harbou
2 Josef von Sternberg	**b** Howard Koch
3 Mitchell Leisen	**c** Mardik Martin
4 Michael Curtiz	**d** Robert Riskin
5 D. W. Griffith	**e** Alma Reville
6 Frank Capra	**f** Preston Sturges
7 George Cukor	**g** Anita Loos
8 Martin Scorsese	**h** Burt Kennedy
9 Alfred Hitchcock	**i** Jules Furthman
10 Fritz Lang	**j** Garson Kanin

■ **109.** What film version of one of his plays did Tennessee Williams consider the best adaptation of his work ever done for the screen?

■ **110.** Raymond Chandler's choice to play Philip Marlowe in the movies was (a) Humphrey Bogart (b) George Raft (c) Cary Grant (d) Jimmy Cagney (e) Laurence Olivier.

■ **111.** Match the films in Column A with the novels on which they were based in Column B:

COLUMN A	COLUMN B
1 Jean-Luc Godard's *Pierrot le fou*	**a** Alberto Moravia's *A Ghost at Noon*
2 Karel Reisz's *Who'll Stop the Rain*	**b** James M. Cain's *The Postman Always Rings Twice*
3 George Stevens's *A Place in the Sun*	**c** Theodore Dreiser's *An American Tragedy*

4 Don Siegel's *The Gun Runners* and Michael Curtiz's *The Breaking Point*

5 Luchino Visconti's *Ossessione* and Pierre Chenal's *Le Dernier tournant*

6 John Ford's *Dr. Bull*

7 John Boulting's *Young Scarface*

8 John Ford's *The Fugitive*

9 Jean-Luc Godard's *Contempt*

10 Douglas Sirk's *A Time to Love and a Time to Die*

d James Gould Cozzens's *The Last Adam*

e Lionel White's *Obsession*

f Graham Greene's *The Power and the Glory*

g Erich Maria Remarque's *A Time to Live and a Time to Die*

h Graham Greene's *Brighton Rock*

i Ernest Hemingway's *To Have and Have Not*

j Robert Stone's *Dog Soldiers*

■ **112.** An ardent admirer of American films and literature, he changed his last name from Grumbach to that of a famous American author. In 1950, he directed a film based on Jean Cocteau's *Les Enfants terrible*. By the mid-fifties, however, this spiritual father to and major influence on the French New Wave was making mostly crime movies (*Bob le flameur*, *Le Doulos*, *The Samurai*), many of them terrific. Name the director.

■ **113.** A segment from a film in Column A appears in a film from Column B. Match them.

Column A

1 Vincente Minnelli's *The Bad and the Beautiful*

Column B

a Jean-Luc Godard's *Contempt*

2 Roger Corman's *Tomb of Ligeia*

3 Howard Hawks's *Red River*

4 Howard Hawks's *The Thing From Another World*

5 George Hill's *Hell Divers*

6 Joseph H. Lewis's *Gun Crazy*

7 Roberto Rossellini's *Voyage in Italy*

8 Michael Anderson's *The Dam Busters*

9 Laslo Benedek's *The Wild One*

10 Fritz Lang's *Metropolis*

b Jacques Rivette's *Paris Belongs to Us*

c Alan Parker's *Pink Floyd: The Wall*

d Martin Scorsese's *Mean Streets*

e Vincente Minnelli's *Two Weeks in Another Town*

f John Carpenter's *Halloween*

g John Ford's *The Wings of Eagles*

h Kenneth Anger's *Scorpio Rising*

i Peter Bogdanovich's *The Last Picture Show*

j Jim McBride's *Breathless*

■ **114.** Name the Polish actress, a suicide in 1971, who, for the movies, created a new last name by combining the first names of Darryl and Virginia Zanuck.

■ **115.** His first film, a masterpiece, had just been released, and he was busy directing and cutting his second. His contract with RKO called for a third film, but he was already looking past that and wanted to get it out of the way quickly. He chose an Eric Ambler thriller, decided not to direct it himself but to oversee someone else's work. He included his manager, secretary, chauffeur, cook, writing assistants, and publicity men—none of them actors—in the cast. Jack Moss, the *wunderkind's* manager, was so terrified by the idea of acting that he agreed to play the picture's villain only after being assured that he wouldn't have to speak a word of dialogue. Name the film and the two directors involved.

P O S T E R   A D   L I N E S

Name the films being advertised:

116. "Notorious Laurie Starr! ... wanted in a dozen states ... hunted by the F.B.I.! She was more than any man could handle!"

117. "A town—a stranger—and the things he does to its people. Especially its women!"

■ **118.** "Chaplin changes! Can you?"

119. "In the future, cities will become deserts, roads will become battlefields, and the hope of mankind will appear as a stranger."

120. "A film on prostitution about a lovely Parisian shopgirl who gives her body but keeps her soul."

121. "It begins with the shriek of a train whistle and ends with shrieking excitement! Young America's idol—a good looking stranger in search of sensation—and a girl in love."

122. " 'I've been wanting to laugh in your face ever since I met you. You're old and ugly and I'm sick of you—sick, sick, sick!' "

123. "A Hollywood story."

124. " 'I just killed my wife and my mother. I know they'll get me. But before that, many more will die. . . .' "

■ **125.** "What do you do when 'the other man' is a woman?"

QUIZ TWO

☆ ☆ ☆

M E M O R A B L E   L I N E S

Name the films in which the following lines appear as well as the actors who spoke them.

■ **126.** "It has always seemed to me that the cocktail should approach us on tiptoe, like a young girl whose first appeal is—innocence."

■ **127.** "What a pity that one ever has to come out-of-doors. Inside, when the curtain is closed, it's possible to forget the present, turn your back to the future, and face the past with hope and confidence."

■ **128.** "The only difference between a derelict and a man is a job."

■ **129.** "I want you to make an investigation and prepare me a report. . I'm serious. It's me I want you to investigate. . . . I'm going to tell you a story, a poetic little story. It's winter of twenty-seven. One night, one snowy night, I found myself a young man in Zurich. I had nothing, nothing, only the one suit I was wearing and a wallet in which there were two hundred thousand Swiss francs. With

32

that money, my fortune was built. You see, I promised you this was poetic. . . . The question is, who was I? . . . What happened before the winter of twenty-seven? Where did I come from in my one suit? That is my real secret, and you are the first man I ever told it to. I do not know who I am!"

■ **130.** "Give me three lines of a man's handwriting, and I will hang him."

☆ ☆ ☆

■ **131.** Mae West was the first choice for the Gloria Swanson role in Billy Wilder's *Sunset Boulevard*. True or false?

■ **132.** Former bootleggers Frank and Maurice King produced a 1945 gangster movie for which they bought the armored-car-robbery footage from Fritz Lang's *You Only Live Once*. Name the film.

■ **133.** Match the directors in Column A and the scriptwriters with whom they often worked in Column B:

COLUMN A	COLUMN B
1 Ernst Lubitsch	**a** Gerard Brach
2 Federico Fellini	**b** Tullio Pinelli
3 Roberto Rossellini	**c** Suso Cecchi d'Amico
4 Jean-Luc Godard	**d** Paul Gégauff
5 Robert Aldrich	**e** Samson Raphaelson
6 Claude Chabrol	**f** Tonino Guerra
7 Roman Polanski	**g** Lukas Heller
8 James Ivory	**h** Jean-Pierre Gorin
9 Luchino Visconti	**i** Federico Fellini
10 Michelangelo Antonioni	**j** Ruth Prawer Jhabvala

■ **134.** Name the producer who yelled: "You call this a script? Give me a couple of five-thousand-dollar-a-week writers and I'll write it myself!"

■ **135.** When Howard Hawks said, "I don't think there's any doubt that she was the best actress I ever worked with," he was talking about (a) Jean Arthur (b) Katharine Hepburn (c) Lauren Bacall (d) Carole Lombard (e) Frances Farmer.

■ **136.** Match the actors and films in Column A with the original choices for the roles in Column B:

COLUMN A	COLUMN B
1 Lamberto Maggiorani in Vittorio De Sica's *The Bicycle Thief*	**a** Montgomery Clift
2 Farley Granger in Luchino Visconti's *Senso*	**b** José Ferrer
3 Peter O'Toole in David Lean's *Lawrence of Arabia*	**c** Cary Grant
4 Dudley Moore in Blake Edwards's *"10"*	**d** Marlon Brando
5 Warren Beatty in George Stevens's *The Only Game in Town*	**e** Frank Sinatra
6 William Holden in Billy Wilder's *Sunset Boulevard*	**f** George Segal
7 Dustin Hoffman in Mike Nichols's *The Graduate*	**g** Albert Finney
8 Ray Milland in Billy Wilder's *The Lost Weekend*	**h** Robert Redford

■ **137.** Name the American director who, when he was only twenty-one, won an Oscar while still in film school. For what movie?

■ **138.** Match the films in Column A (all remakes) with those in Column B (the original versions):

COLUMN A

1 Frank Tashlin's *Rock-a-Bye Baby*

2 Robert Z. Leonard's *In the Good Old Summertime*

3 George Cukor's *Rich and Famous*

4 Howard Hawks's *A Song Is Born*

5 John Cromwell's *Algiers*

6 Frank Capra's *A Pocketful of Miracles*

7 Charles Marquis Warren's *Hellgate*

8 Norman Taurog's *Living It Up*

9 Tim Whelan's *Step Lively*

10 Dick Powell's *You Can't Run Away From It*

COLUMN B

a Frank Capra's *It Happened One Night*

b Preston Sturges's *The Miracle of Morgan's Creek*

c Julien Duvivier's *Pépé le Moko*

d Frank Capra's *Lady for a Day*

e John Ford's *The Prisoner of Shark Island*

f William Wellman's *Nothing Sacred*

g Howard Hawks's *Ball of Fire*

h the Marx Brothers's *Room Service*

i Vincent Sherman's *Old Acquaintance*

j Ernst Lubitsch's *The Shop Around the Corner*

■ **139.** "Mother of God, is this the end of Rico?" Edward G. Robinson asks at the close of Mervyn LeRoy's *Little Caesar.* Or is it "Mother of mercy, is this the end of Rico?"

■ **140.** Name the director who, during the filming of an especially spectacular scene, casually said to his assistant, "Move those ten thousand horses a trifle to the right."

■ **141.** Name the only movie in which John, Lionel, and Ethel Barrymore starred together.

■ **142.** Match the title of the film in Column A with its working title in Column B:

COLUMN A	COLUMN B
1 Billy Wilder's *Ace in the Hole/The Big Carnival*	**a** *Sleep No More*
2 John Ford's *The Whole Town's Talking*	**b** *Miracle on 49th Street*
3 Robert Rossen's *Body and Soul*	**c** *An Affair of the Heart*
4 Don Siegel's *Dirty Harry*	**d** *Homicide*
5 Jules Dassin's *The Naked City*	**e** *The Human Interest Story*
6 Ben Hecht's and Charles MacArthur's *The Scoundrel*	**f** *Diamonds in the Pavement*
7 Don Siegel's *Invasion of the Body Snatchers*	**g** *Golden Warriors*
8 Elia Kazan's *On the Waterfront*	**h** *Passport to Fame*
9 The Marx Brothers' *Love Happy*	**i** *The Whip Master*
10 Elia Kazan's *Baby Doll*	**j** *Dead Right*

■ **143.** Speaking of working titles, Nicholas Ray claimed he used the same one for every film he directed. What was it?

☆ ☆ ☆

Each decade since the early fifties, the British film magazine *Sight & Sound* has asked a number of the world's film critics for a list of their top ten—but not necessarily "best"—films of all time. *Sight & Sound* then counts the votes and publishes the results. Thus far, five top-ten lists have appeared—in 1952, 1962, 1972, 1982, and 1992. There have also been four lists naming the critics' top-ten directors—in 1962, 1972, 1982, and 1992. The next seven questions are about the *Sight & Sound* polls.

■ **144.** Only two films have appeared on all five *Sight & Sound* top-ten lists. Which are they: (a) Orson Welles's *Citizen Kane* (b) D. W. Griffith's *The Birth of a Nation* (c) Jean Renoir's *La Règle du jeu* (d) Sergei Eisenstein's *Battleship Potemkin* (e) Erich von Stroheim's *Greed* (f) Charlie Chaplin's *City Lights*?

145. Name the film that's topped the *Sight & Sound* top-ten lists since 1962.

146. Only one musical has ever made a *Sight & Sound* top-ten list. Name it.

■ **147.** Name the most current film—the year was 1968—on the 1992 *Sight & Sound* top-ten list.

■ **148.** Only four color films have ever appeared on a *Sight & Sound* list, and then not until 1982. Which are they: (a) Max Ophuls's *Lola Montés* (b) Martin Scorsese's *Taxi Driver* (c) John Ford's *The Searchers* (d) Vincente Minnelli's *An American in Paris* (e) Alfred Hitchcock's *Vertigo* (f) Stanley Donen's and Gene Kelly's *Singin' in the Rain* (g) Stanley Kubrick's *2001: A Space Odyssey*?

149. Who is the only director with two films on the 1972 *Sight & Sound* top-ten list? Name the films.

— **150.** Which of the following directors are included in the critics' 1992 *Sight & Sound* top-ten directors list: (a) François Truffaut (b) Michelangelo

Antonioni (c) Howard Hawks (d) D. W. Griffith (e) Ernst Lubitsch (f) F. W. Murnau (g) Max Ophuls (h) Josef von Sternberg (i) Erich von Stroheim (j) Luchino Visconti (k) Ingmar Bergman (l) Roberto Rossellini (m) Kenji Mizoguchi (n) Andrej Wajda (o) Marcel Carné (p) Robert Bresson (q) Jean Vigo (r) Fritz Lang (s) Georges Franju (t) Vittorio De Sica (u) Martin Scorsese (v) Werner Herzog (w) Alain Resnais (x) Preston Sturges (y) Andrei Tarkovsky (z) Frank Capra?

P O S T E R   A D   L I N E S

Name the films being advertised:

151. "People are the ultimate spectacle."

152. "Not a man . . . not an animal . . ."

153. "This is the weekend they didn't play golf."

154. "It's no laughing matter."

155. " 'I killed my father, I ate human flesh and I quiver with joy.' "

156. "When she was good she was very very good. When she was bad, she was . . ."

157. "A comedy about love, death, and freedom."

158. "The frank and shocking story of the world's most famous woman of scandal! She lived too intensely and far too well!"

159. "There were three men in her life. One to take her . . . one to love her—and one to kill her."

160. "Raging island! Raging passions! This is IT!"

QUIZ THREE

Name the films in which these memorable opening lines appear as well as the actors who spoke them:

■ **161.** "I am packing my belongings in the shawl my mother used to wear when she went to the market, and I am going from my valley. And this time, I shall never return."

■ **162.** "There was me—that is, Alex—and my three droogs—that is, Pete, Georgie and Dim—and we sat in the Korova, trying to make up our rassoodocks what to do with the evening."

■ **163.** "The Sengoku Period was a time of civil wars; it was a lawless era and in the country the farmers were at the mercy of bands of brigands."

■ **164.** "On Sunday, August thirteenth, 1961, the eyes of America were on the nation's capital where Roger Maris was hitting home runs number forty-four and forty-five against the Senators. On that same day, without any warning, the East German Communists sealed off the border between East and West

Berlin. I only mention this to show the kind of people we're dealing with—real shifty."

■ **165.** "The past is a foreign country. They do things differently there."

☆ ☆ ☆

■ **166.** Her disappearance early in the film is what propels the plot and makes the film so haunting. Rumor has it that the director had the use of the actress for only three days, so he was forced to make her absence fit the story. Name the actress, the director, and the film.

■ **167.** Directors Sam Fuller and Budd Boetticher first met when they served together in the First Infantry Division during World War II. After the war, both men wrote novels about their combat experiences. Astonishingly, the books had the same title: *The Big Red One*. Though Fuller and Boetticher remained friends, Fuller's agent sued Boetticher when the latter announced he was going to make a movie called *The Big Red One*. Fuller had similar plans. Boetticher lost the case, and his book was eventually filmed in 1962 as *Hell Is for Heroes*, directed by Don Siegel. True or false?

■ **168.** Match the author in Column A with his or her autobiography or book of memoirs in Column B:

COLUMN A	COLUMN B
1 Josef von Sternberg	**a** *A Tree Is a Tree*
2 Lillian Hellman	**b** *My Wicked, Wicked Ways*
3 King Vidor	**c** *Fun in a Chinese Laundry*
4 Ben Hecht	**d** *Scoundrel Time*
5 Errol Flynn	**e** *Goodness Had Nothing to Do With It*
6 Mae West	**f** *A Child of the Century*

■ **169.** Formed in 1917 to revamp Germany's world image, this studio was bought by a bank after World War I and put under the leadership of Erich Pommer, the producer of *The Cabinet of Dr. Caligari.* Because of competition from Hollywood, the studio was almost bankrupt by the end of the twenties when it was rescued by a group of Nazi sympathizers. Much of its product thus became propaganda, although apolitical films such as Josef von Sternberg's *The Blue Angel* (based on Heinrich Mann's novel) were occasionally produced. During World War II, Joseph Goebbels assumed direct control. In 1945, everything went kaput. Name the studio.

■ **170.** Name the only two actors to receive Oscars for playing the same character. In what film or films?

C O M M O N A L I T I E S

■ **171.** What role do the following actresses have in common: Renée Falconetti, Jean Seberg, Florence Delay, Ingrid Bergman, and Ingrid Bergman?

■ **172.** What do the following movies have in common: Mark Robson's *The Harder They Fall*, Stanley Kramer's *Guess Who's Coming to Dinner*, Raoul Levy's *The Defector*, Michael Anderson's *The Naked Edge*, and Don Siegel's *The Shootist*?

■ **173.** What do the following directors have in common: George Stevens, Victor Fleming, Rudolph Maté, William Fraker, and Guy Green?

■ **174.** What do the following movies have in common: John Ford's *The Horse Soldiers*, John Huston's *The Red Badge of Courage*, Sergio Leone's *The Good, the*

Bad and the Ugly, Buster Keaton's and Clyde Bruckman's *The General*, and D. W. Griffith's *The Birth of a Nation?*

■ **175.** What do the following movies have in common: Peter Yates's *Bullitt*, Don Siegel's *The Lineup*, William Friedkin's *The French Connection*, Philip D'Antoni's *The Seven-Ups*, and Walter Hill's *The Driver?*

☆ ☆ ☆

■ **176.** Name the major Alfred Hitchcock film in which a known murderer escapes punishment and isn't even seen during the picture's final forty or so minutes.

■ **177.** In the thirties, the Japanese coined the term—in English—to describe the films of Yasujiro Shimazu. Then, in the June 1943 issue of *Il Film*, Italian critic Umberto Barbaro used the same term while writing about French director Marcel Carné's *Quai des brumes*. Soon after, it was applied to one of the most important movements in cinema history, a movement whose credo was "Let's make a film: a man looks for work." What is the term?

■ **178.** Match the films in Column A with their dedications in Column B:

COLUMN A	COLUMN B
1 François Truffaut's *Stolen Kisses*	**a** The French Cinémathèque and Henry Langlois
2 Jacques Demy's *Lola*	**b** Jean-Pierre Léaud
3 François Truffaut's *The Wild Child*	**c** To the people who first suggested that it be made—

librarian Jo Ellen Misakian and the students of the Lone Star School in Fresno, California

4 Jean-Luc Godard's *Made in U.S.A*

d Max Ophuls

5 William Wellman's *Roxie Hart*

e To Nick and Samuel, whose pupil I am in terms of sight and sound

6 Francis Coppola's *The Outsiders*

f To all the beautiful women in the world who shot their men full of holes out of pique

■ **179.** George Lucas "borrowed" the plot of *Star Wars* from what classic Japanese film: (a) Yasujiro Ozu's *Tokyo Story* (b) Akira Kurosawa's *Yojimbo* (c) Akira Kurosawa's *Seven Samurai* (d) Kenji Mizoguchi's *Ugetsu* (e) Akira Kurosawa's *The Hidden Fortress*?

■ **180.** Sergio Leone's *A Fistful of Dollars*, starring Clint Eastwood, was based on one of the five Japanese films listed in the preceding question. Which one?

L A S T   L I N E S

Name the films in which these memorable closing lines appear as well as the actors who spoke them:

■ **181.** "All right, Mr. DeMille, I'm ready for my close-up."

■ **182.** "The ashes were collected in urns and put into a pigeonhole which was then sealed up. . . . Catherine had always wished hers to be scattered to the winds from the top of a hill, but it was not allowed."

■ **183.** "Yowsa, yowsa, yowsa! Here they are again— these wonderful, wonderful kids, still struggling, still hoping, as the clock of fate ticks away. The dance of destiny continues. The marathon goes on and on and on. How long can they last? Let's hear it. Come on, let's hear it. Let's hear it. Let's hear it."

■ **184.** "You know something, Fanny? I wouldn't tell this to anybody but you, but it seemed to me as if someone else was in that room, and that, through me, she'd brought her boy under shelter again, and that I'd been true at last to my very true love."

■ **185.** "Mein Führer, I can walk!"

QUIZ THREE

★ ★

F I R S T   L I N E S

Name the films in which these memorable opening lines appear as well as the actors who spoke them:

- **186.** "It begins here for me on this road."

- **187.** "Children believe what we tell them, they have complete faith in us. They believe a rose plucked from a garden can bring drama to a family. They believe the hands of a human beast will smoke when he slays a victim, and the beast will be ashamed when confronted with a young girl. They believe a thousand other simple things."

- **188.** "You said to me: I love you. I said to you: Wait. I was going to say: Take me. You said to me: Go away."

- **189.** "But he gave them to me on our wedding day. What shall I do?"

- **190.** "You see? You see the symbolism of it? Capital and labor destroy each other! It teaches a lesson, a moral lesson. It has social significance!"

★ ★ ★

45

■ **191.** John Wayne died of cancer in 1979. In the fifties, he starred in a movie that was filmed in Saint George, Utah, only 137 miles from Yucca Flats, Nevada, where above-ground nuclear testing had taken place. Since about half of the film's 220 cast and crew members later contracted cancer—many of them dying of it—there would seem to be a connection between the movie's locale and the disease. The film was (a) Henry Hathaway's *Legend of the Lost* (b) John Ford's *The Searchers* (c) Dick Powell's *The Conqueror* (d) Howard Hawks's *Rio Bravo* (e) John Farrow's *Hondo*.

■ **192.** Nominated for a Best Supporting Actress Oscar six times in thirteen years, this Brooklyn-born star was one of Hollywood's best character actresses in the forties, fifties, and sixties, working with Joseph L. Mankiewicz, Sam Fuller, Alfred Hitchcock, Frank Capra, and John Huston. She usually played a wisecracker with a heart of gold. Name the actress.

■ **193.** Match the author in Column A with his autobiography or book of memoirs in Column B:

COLUMN A	COLUMN B
1 Edward Dmytryk	**a** *My Life in Pictures*
2 Jean Renoir	**b** *My Life and My Films*
3 Frank Capra	**c** *I Remember It Well*
4 Budd Schulberg	**d** *It's a Hell of a Life But Not a Bad Living*
5 Charlie Chaplin	**e** *The Name Above the Title*
6 Vincente Minnelli	**f** *Moving Pictures*

■ **194.** Ingmar Bergman used short clips of a skeleton and an executioner from *Prison/The Devil's Wanton* (1949) in one of his later films. It was (a) *Cries and*

Whispers (b) *Persona* (c) *The Magic Flute* (d) *Fanny and Alexander* (e) *The Magician*?

■ **195.** How does Maida Vale figure prominently in the only film that Alfred Hitchcock shot in 3-D (though it wasn't widely released that way)? Name the picture.

C O M M O N A L I T I E S

What do the following groups of films have in common:

■ **196.** Ben Hecht's *Actors and Sin*, Howard Hawks's *The Big Sky*, John Huston's *A Walk With Love and Death*, Alfred Hitchcock's *Strangers on a Train*, Vincente Minnelli's *A Matter of Time*.

■ **197.** Jean-Luc Godard's *A Woman Is a Woman*, Orson Welles's *The Immortal Story*, Alfred Hitchcock's *Rope*, Jean Renoir's *The River*, Ingmar Bergman's *Now About All These Women*, John Ford's *Drums Along the Mohawk*.

■ **198.** Roman Polanski's *Chinatown*, Jean-Luc Godard's *Contempt*, Jean-Luc Godard's *Pierrot le fou*, Milos Forman's *Hair*, Charlie Chaplin's *Limelight*, Max Ophuls's *The Earrings of Madame de* . . .

■ **199.** Robert Aldrich's *The Big Knife*, William Wyler's *The Big Country*, Otto Preminger's *Bunny Lake Is Missing*, John Frankenheimer's *Seconds*, Stanley Kubrick's *Spartacus*, Alfred Hitchcock's *Vertigo*, Billy Wilder's *The Seven Year Itch*.

■ **200.** Haskell Wexler's *Medium Cool*, Ken Russell's *The Devils*, Stanley Kubrick's *A Clockwork Orange*, John Schlesinger's *Midnight Cowboy*, Bernardo Bertolucci's *Last Tango in Paris*.

☆ ☆ ☆

■ **201.** When Orson Welles arrived in Hollywood in 1939, he planned to make a film of Joseph Conrad's *Heart of Darkness* (in which he'd play both Kurtz and Marlow). When the project fell through, he wrote scripts based on Nicholas Blake's *The Smiler With a Knife* and Arthur Calder Marshall's *The Way to Santiago*, both thrillers. For various reasons, neither film got off the ground. Then—and only then—came *Citizen Kane*. True or false?

■ **202.** The St. Valentine's Day Massacre was first depicted in (a) Josef von Sternberg's *Underworld* (b) Josef von Sternberg's *Thunderbolt* (c) Rouben Mamoulian's *City Streets* (d) Howard Hawks's *Scarface* (e) Nicholas Ray's *Party Girl*?

■ **203.** Match the films in Column A with their dedications in Column B:

COLUMN A	COLUMN B
1 Sam Fuller's *The Steel Helmet*	**a** Monogram Pictures
2 Jean-Luc Godard's *Breathless*	**b** To the memory of those who made us laugh: the motley mountebanks, the clowns, the buffoons, in all times and in nations, whose efforts have lightened our burden a little, this picture is affectionately dedicated.
3 John Ford's *3 Godfathers*	**c** To the memory of Harry Carey—bright star of the Western sky.
4 Ridley Scott's *Blade Runner*	**d** The United States Infantry

5 Preston Sturges's **e** To the memory of
   Sullivan's Travels   Philip K. Dick

■ **204.** Though he was a real dog, his movies weren't—
for years they practically saved the studio he
worked for. He always received top billing over
mere humans, and his scripts were often written
by Darryl F. Zanuck. Since his bark was as good as
his bite, he had no trouble moving from the silent
era into sound films. Name him.

■ **205.** Match the well-known writer in Column A with
the film that he or she directed in Column B:

COLUMN A	COLUMN B
1 Curzio Malaparte	**a** *Portnoy's Complaint*
2 Thomas McGuane	**b** *Days in the Trees*
3 Norman Mailer	**c** *Duet for Cannibals*
4 Ben Hecht	**d** *92° in the Shade*
5 George Axelrod	**e** *Strange Deception*
6 Ernest Lehman	**f** *Lord Love a Duck*
7 Clifford Odets	**g** *Maidstone*
8 Susan Sontag	**h** *None But the Lonely Heart*
9 Marguerite Duras	**i** *Force of Evil*
10 Abraham Polonsky	**j** *Specter of the Rose*

L A S T   L I N E S

Name the films in which these memorable closing lines
appear as well as the actors who spoke them:

■ **206.** "Ain't like it used to be, but it'll do."

■ **207.** "It's sad when a mother has to speak the words
that condemn her own son. But I couldn't allow
them to believe that I would commit murder.
They'll put him away now, as I should have years

ago. He was always bad and, in the end, he intended to tell them I killed those girls and that man. As if I could do anything except sit and stare like one of his stuffed birds. Oh, they know I can't even move a finger, and I won't. I'll just sit here and be quiet, just in case they do suspect me. They're probably watching me. Well, let them. Let them see what kind of a person I am. I'm not even going to swat that fly. I hope they *are* watching. They'll see. They'll see and they'll know and they'll say, 'Why she wouldn't even harm a fly.' "

■ **208.** "A slut up there and a slut down here, and what's more, the sea is a traitor. How can a man live like this?"

■ **209.** [Boys sing]
"Hark, an angel bears its light
Through the gates of heaven.
By God's angel's beams so bright
All the black nocturnal shades are
driven."

■ **210.** "Arrested on October 12, 1944. Tried by a military court of the Resistance, he was sentenced to death and executed."

QUIZ THREE

☆ ☆ ☆

F I R S T   L I N E S

Name the films in which these memorable opening lines appear as well as the actors who spoke them:

■ **211.** "I forgot the opening line."

■ **212.** "I was born here in the shanties, on the outskirts of Warsaw. I grew up in poverty. I made my first friends here, had my first lessons. I had a tough time when I was a kid because I didn't know my friends from my enemies. I had too much confidence in myself—my legs and fists. My ma tried to keep a pretty firm hold over me, trying to push me off to work. But I treated it like typical woman's nagging. I preferred playing knives with my pals instead. ... That wasn't all we did. In 1942, supplies for the German army were being transported by train. I used to throw coal down from the cars—a patriotic thief."

■ **213.** "Every afternoon at exactly the same time, I start my tour of duty by driving down the Champs-Elysées."

■ **214.** "This is Wall Street, and today was important because tomorrow, July Fourth, I intended to make my first million dollars, an exciting day in any man's life."

■ **215.** "You don't make up your sins in church. You do it in the streets. You do it at home. The rest is bullshit, and you know it."

☆ ☆ ☆

■ **216.** Match the blacklisted writer in Column A with the pseudonym he used for the film in parenthesis in Column B:

COLUMN A	COLUMN B
1 Donald Ogden Stewart	**a** H. B. Addis (Luis Buñuel's *The Young One*)
2 Dalton Trumbo	**b** Peter Howard (Joseph Losey's *A Finger of Guilt/The Innocent Stranger*)
3 Ben Hecht	**c** Gilbert Holland (Philip Leacock's *Escapade*)
4 Ring Lardner Jr.	**d** Philip Rush (Pat Jackson's *Virgin Island*)
5 Hugo Butler	**e** Robert Rich (Irving Rapper's *The Brave One*)
6 Lester Cole	**f** Derek Frye (Joseph Losey's *The Sleeping Tiger*)
7 Carl Foreman	**g** Lester Bartow (Otto Preminger's *Whirlpool*)
8 Howard Koch	**h** Gerald L. C. Copley (James Hill's *Born Free*)

■ **217.** The Italian cinémathèque was founded by directors Alberto Lattuada and Luigi Comencini. The French Cinémathèque was founded by Henri

Langlois and a famous French director. Name him.

■ **218.** Match the author in Column A with his or her autobiography or book of memoirs in Column B:

Column A	Column B
1 Frances Marion	**a** *Each Man in His Time*
2 Mervyn LeRoy	**b** *Hollywood Red*
3 Philip Dunne	**c** *Whatever Happened to Hollywood?*
4 Lester Cole	**d** *Off With Their Heads*
5 Jesse Lasky Jr.	**e** *Take One*
6 Raoul Walsh	**f** *Take Two*

■ **219.** Henry Fonda's acting career got started when he was asked to join the Omaha Community Playhouse by the mother of a then one-year-old son who would grow up to be an actor fully as famous as Fonda. Name him.

■ **220.** Though the plot isn't totally identical, this midsixties horror movie seems to be based on Tennessee Williams's *Suddenly, Last Summer*. Name it.

C O M M O N A L I T I E S

What do the following groups of films have in common:

■ **221.** Max Ophuls's *Liebelei*, Alfred Hitchcock's *Vertigo*, Michael Powell's and Emeric Pressburger's *Black Narcissus*, Louis Malle's *A Very Private Affair*, François Truffaut's *Shoot the Piano Player*, Robert Bresson's *Une Femme douce*.

■ **222.** Jacques Tourneur's *Wichita*, Sam Peckinpah's *Pat Garrett & Billy the Kid*, Monte Hellman's *China 9, Liberty 37*, Don Siegel's *Invasion of the Body Snatchers*.

■ **223.** Milos Forman's *Ragtime*, Arthur Penn's *Four Friends*, John Boorman's *Deliverance*, Ben Hecht's and Charles MacArthur's *Crime Without Passion*, Warren Beatty's *Reds*.

■ **224.** Akira Kurosawa's *High and Low*, Howard Hawks's *Fig Leaves*, William Dieterle's *Portrait of Jennie*, Martin Scorsese's *Raging Bull*, Andrei Tarkovsky's *Andrei Rublev*.

■ **225.** Sam Peckinpah's *Cross of Iron* and *The Wild Bunch*, John Huston's *The Treasure of the Sierra Madre*, and *Beat the Devil*, Preston Sturges's *Sullivan's Travels*, Joseph L. Mankiewicz's *5 Fingers*.

☆ ☆ ☆

■ **226.** What remarkable musical family can claim two uncles and a nephew as film composer-conductors? Name all three, if you can.

■ **227.** Best known for her portrayals in fifties *noir* films, she married both a famous director and his son, thereby becoming the director's daughter-in-law after being the son's stepmother. Name the actress, the director, and the director's son.

■ **228.** Match the films in Column A with their dedications in Column B:

COLUMN A	COLUMN B
1 Martin Scorsese's *Raging Bull*	**a** Dan Johnson
2 Wim Wenders's *Wings of Desire*	**b** Haig P. Manoogian
3 Martin Scorsese's *The King of Comedy*	**c** The Kinks

4 Wim Wenders's *Summer in the City*   **d** to all the former angels but especially to Yasujiro, François, and Andrej

■ **229.** Max Ophuls's *Letter From an Unknown Woman* is a glorious film, but Alfred Hitchcock, not Ophuls, was producer John Houseman's first choice to direct Stefan Zweig's bittersweet story, and we can thank David O. Selznick for nixing the idea. True or false?

■ **230.** Jean-Paul Sartre and Simone de Beauvoir didn't go to see Jean Renoir's classic *La Grand Illusion* when it opened in France in 1937 because (a) they considered Renoir a bourgeois reactionary with no concept of Marxism (b) they had relocated to London because they knew a major war with Germany was not far off (c) they refused to see films featuring men in uniform (d) there was no cartoon before the film (e) they weren't sympathetic with what they termed Renoir's "anarcho-Christian, pseudo-mystical sentimentalism"?

L A S T   L I N E S

Name the films in which these memorable closing lines appear as well as the actors who spoke them:

■ **231.** "You can tell me. You knew him better that I did. Was he going away with her? I have to know. Was he going away with her?"

■ **232.** " 'Neither the sun nor death can be faced steadily.' "

■ **233.** "Well, everybody is somebody s fool The only way to stay out of trouble is to grow old, so I guess I'll concentrate on that Maybe I'll live so long that I'll forget her. Maybe I'll die trying."

■ **234.** "I know she's there. Maybe someday I'll find her Maybe I'll die trying."

■ **235.** "Gaff had been there—and let her live. Four years he figured. He was wrong. Tyrell had told me Rachael was special: no termination date I didn't know how long we'd have together. Who does?"

QUIZ FOUR
☆

Name the films in which the following lines appear as well as the actors who spoke them:

■ **236.** "Now listen, Mike Listen carefully. I'm going to pronounce a few words. They're harmless words—just a bunch of letters scrambled together—but their meaning is important. Try to understand what they mean. Manhattan Project. Los Alamos Trinity."

■ **237.** "I've seen guys like you go under before. Guys that never had a worry. Then they got ahold of some dough and went goofy.   The first thing that happens to a guy like that, he starts wanting to go into restaurants and sit down at a table and eat salads and cupcakes and tea. Boy, what that kind of food does to your system! And the next thing the dope wants is a room. Yes sir, a room with steam heat and curtains and rugs, and afore you know it, he's all softened up and can't sleep unless'n he has a bed. . . . I've seen plenty of guys start out with fifty bucks and wind up with a bank account. . . . And let me tell you, Long John, when you become a guy with a bank account, they got you. Yes sir, they got you."

■ **238.** "There's a Foreign Legion of women too. But we have no uniforms, no flags, and no medals when we are brave. No wound stripes when we are hurt."

■ **239.** "Have you sublet this apartment? You're here often enough to pay rent. . . . Haven't you any sense of privacy? . . . Have detectives who buy portraits of murder victims a claim to privacy? Lancaster Corey told me that you've already put in a bid for it. . . . McPherson, did it ever strike you that you're acting very strangely? It's a wonder you don't come here like a suitor with roses and a box of candy. Drugstore candy, of course. . . . You better watch out, McPherson, or you'll wind up in a psychiatric ward. I don't think they've ever had a patient who fell in love with a corpse."

■ **240.** "You will come. There is only the desert for you."

☆ ☆ ☆

■ **241.** Because of his notorious dislike of cigarette and cigar smoke, Alfred Hitchcock once planned to have the hero in one of his films—a man who also hated smoking—tortured into revealing crucial information by placing him in a small, smoke-filled room in which the villains puffed huge cigars while playing cards. Hitchcock's producer, who loved Cuban cigars, took the scene as a personal insult and made the director change the method of torture. True or false?

■ **242.** In 1953, Georges Sadoul, the respected French film historian, wrote: "This discreet, commercially unsuccessful and therefore, unfortunately, little known film marked the turning point in [the director's] life, and at the same time can be traced as the source from which springs the modern Italian school of Rossellini and de Sica." Sadoul is talking about (a) Marcel Carné's *Le Jour se lève* (b) Jean Renoir's *Toni* (c) Max Ophuls's *Une Histoire d'amour* (d) Jean Cocteau's *The Blood of a Poet* (e) Jean Renoir's *The Crime of Monsieur Lange?*

■ **243.** Name the New York City-born actor who worked briefly as a female impersonator before conquering Vaudeville, Broadway, and Hollywood. In what famous crime movies does he shove a grapefruit in a woman's face and sit in his mother's lap? He retired in 1961 but made a comeback twenty years later, playing a top cop in a prestigious, rather empty picture. Name it.

■ **244.** At first, it sounded like an unnecessary gimmick— a Western with four sets of brothers playing four sets of brothers—but the idea arguably added even more verisimilitude to one of our last good Westerns. Name the movie and the actors.

■ **245.** What famous American avant-garde film begins with the film's title and the director's name spelled out in silver studs on a black leather motorcycle jacket?

C R I T I C S   O N   F I L M
....

Identify the films and the directors being discussed:

■ **246.** Andrew Sarris: "Perhaps it was all a happy accident, and the lightning of inspiration will never
strike again in the same spot. The fact remains that
[the film] has turned out to be the *Citizen Kane* of
jukebox musicals, the brilliant crystallization of
such diverse cultural particles as the pop movie,
rock 'n' roll, *cinéma vérité*, the *nouvelle vague*, free
cinema, the affectedly handheld camera, frenzied
cutting, the cult of the sexless subadolescent, the
semidocumentary, and studied spontaneity."

■ **247.** Robin Wood: "The directness—the vital, spontaneous frankness—with which the characters confront and attack each other is enormously affecting, because this urgency of contact derives from
their constant (not necessarily conscious) sense of
the imminence of death, of surrounding darkness,
a *physical* intuition that prompts them to live, *now*,
to the maximum. It is partly this that makes [the
director's] films, in fact, so modern: in the world
of the hydrogen bomb, one doesn't have to be an
Andes mailplane flier to feel that one may be dead
tomorrow."

■ **248.** Dwight Macdonald: "This portrait of the artist as
a middle-aged man is the most brilliant, varied
and entertaining movie I've seen since *Citizen
Kane*. . . . I hazard that [the film] is [the director's]
masterpiece precisely because it is about the two
subjects he knows the most about: himself and the
making of movies. He doesn't have to labor his
points, he can move freely, quickly, with the ease
of a man walking about his own home. . . . This fa-

miliarity also means that [the director] is able to keep [the film] right down to earth, so that what might have been one more labored exercise in fantasy—like De Sica's *Miracle in Milan*, for instance— is spontaneous, lifelike and often very funny. I think [the director] has become the greatest master of social comedy since Lubitsch. . . . The offputting quality of [the film] for all but the less intellectualized critics (and the public) is that it is nothing but a pleasurable work of art which might have been directed by Mozart—and there were no doubt pundits in his day who deplored the frivolous way he played around with Masonic symbolism in *The Magic Flute*. . . . This is perhaps the difficulty; nothing for the interpretative tooth to mumble, no Antonionian *angst*, no Bermanesque Godhead, no Truffaut-style existential Absurd to perplex us. Like Baroque art, of which it is a belated golden ray, [the film] is complicated but not obscure. . . . One could drop still another name, the greatest of all. Is there not something Shakespearean in this range of human experience expressed in every mode from high lyric to low comic, from the most formal rhetoric to the most personal impressionism?"

■ **249.** Carlos Clarens: "[The director] directed [the film] from the Clare Boothe play dedicated to the misogynist conceit that a woman's worst enemy is either herself or another woman, possibly her best friend and confidante. . . . Nothing, or very little, remains of Scott Fitzgerald's adaptation except perhaps an excessive concern with the heroine's background and breeding which, since the play was acquired for Norma Shearer, was inevitable from the start. The final screenplay, by Jane Murfin and Anita Loos, is not only funnier than the original but tougher as well. . . . No men are seen or heard anywhere, as in the play, only now this unnatural absence establishes a sort of artificiality which [the director] sustains through countless short scenes and vignettes with a prodigious pace, while allowing now and then a few stinging truths about divorce and children."

■ **250.** Robert Warshow: "In [the film], . . . the legend of the West is virtually reduced to its essentials and then fixed in the dreamy clarity of a fairy tale. There never was so broad and bare and lovely a landscape as [the director] puts before us, or so unimaginably comfortless a 'town' as the little group of buildings on the prairie to which the settlers must come for their supplies and to buy a drink. The mere physical progress of the film . . . is so deliberately graceful that everything seems to be happening at the bottom of a clear lake. The hero . . . is hardly a man at all, but something like the Spirit of the West, beautiful in fringed buckskins. He emerges mysteriously from the plains, breathing sweetness and a melancholy which is no longer simply the Westerner's natural response to experience but has taken on spirituality; and when he has accomplished his mission, meeting and destroying . . . a Spirit of Evil just as metaphysical as his own embodiment of virtue, he fades away again into the more distant West, a man whose 'day is over,' leaving behind the wondering little boy who might have imagined the whole story."

☆ ☆ ☆

■ **251.** Though they all believed he could play a first-rate tough guy, almost everyone in Hollywood had some doubt that Humphrey Bogart could win over audiences as a romantic leading man. Michael Curtiz's *Casablanca*, in which Bogart starred with Ingrid Bergman, was the film that convinced them. True or false?

■ **252.** A famous actress from the silent era—starring in Erich von Stroheim's *Greed*—she continued to work in movies and television into the early sixties. Her first name was derived from one syllable each from the names of her aunts, Eliza and Susan. Name the actress.

■ **253.** Match the film in Column A with its ostensible biographical subject in Column B:

COLUMN A	COLUMN B
1 Albert Lewin's *The Moon and Sixpence*	**a** George M. Cohan
2 Robert Rossen's *All the King's Men*	**b** John Reed
3 Martin Scorsese's *Raging Bull*	**c** Paul Gauguin
4 Orson Welles's *Citizen Kane*	**d** Huey Long
5 Arthur Penn's *The Miracle Worker*	**e** F. Scott Fitzgerald
6 Warren Beatty's *Reds*	**f** Helen Keller
7 Michael Curtiz's *Yankee Doodle Dandy*	**g** William Randolph Hearst
8 Henry King's *Beloved Infidel*	**h** Jake La Motta

■ **254.** He grew up in the tough East Harlem section of New York City. After dropping out of New York University, he and a childhood friend, Nick Cravat, made their living as circus acrobats for almost a decade. Following World War II, he became an actor, moving from Broadway to Hollywood and stardom. Though many of his early movies were crime or adventure films (sometimes featuring Cravat), he quickly proved he could be more than a tough guy doing stunts. He was one of the first actors to become an independent producer (his company produced Delbert Mann's *Marty* in 1955), he made films for such eminent foreign directors as Luchino Visconti (*The Leopard*), and he always displayed a keen eye for serious roles in prestigious, though not always big-budget, films. Name the actor.

■ **255.** Just once have two members of the same family won major Oscars on the same night. Who were they? What awards did they win? For what movie or movies were they honored?

P O S T E R   A D   L I N E S

Name the films being advertised:

■ **256.** "The truest and most human story of the Great White Snows."

■ **257.** "The immortal love story of the gentle clown and the beautiful ballerina."

■ **258.** "François Truffaut has created a new film masterpiece from the only other novel by the author of *Jules and Jim*."

■ **259.** "The nearer they get to their treasure, the farther they get from the law."

■ **260.** "The barbarous love that left Egypt's great pyramid as its wondrous landmark."

■ **261.** "I'm a teacher. My pupils are the kind you don't turn your back on, even in class."

■ **262.** "Doyle is bad news . . . but a good cop!"

■ **263.** " 'As far back as I can remember, I've always wanted to be a gangster.'—Henry Hill, Brooklyn, N.Y., 1955"

■ **264.** "Love never dies."

■ **265.** "He's not Freddy, he's not Jason . . . he's real."

QUIZ FOUR

M E M O R A B L E   L I N E S

Name the films in which the following lines appear as well as the actors who spoke them:

■ **266.** "Always I must walk the streets alone. And always I am followed—soundlessly. Yet I hear it. It's me pursuing myself."

■ **267.** ACTRESS: "Hey, you're sort of a handsome man."

ACTOR: "But I'm not the right man. And neither is he."

ACTRESS: "Maybe not. But it doesn't matter,"

ACTOR: "You don't understand, Jill. People like that have something inside—something to do with death. If that fellow lives, he'll come in through that door, pick up his gear and say adios. It would be nice to see this town grow."

■ **268.** "After the aforesaid Herlof's Marte had been tortured by the executioner to the glory of God, she made a voluntary confession as stated above, and witnessed by us assembled priests. Absalon Pedersøn."

■ **269.** "Well, I lived most of my life in the wild country, and you set a code of laws to live by. . . . I won't be wronged. I won't be insulted, and I won't be laid a hand on. I don't do these things to other people, and I require the same from them."

■ **270.** "You're not too smart, are you? I like that in a man."

☆ ☆ ☆

■ **271.** In what film do Jimmy Stewart and Duke Ellington play the piano together?

■ **272.** In 1928, Erich von Stroheim directed a film that starred (and was produced by) Gloria Swanson. The financing came from robber baron Joseph P. Kennedy, the actress's one-time lover. About halfway through the filming, Swanson fired Stroheim, recut the existing footage and, much to the director's disgust, released the picture in Europe. Americans had never seen any part of the film until a clip from it appeared in a famous 1950 film. Name the two films.

■ **273.** Match the executive in Column A with the film studio with which he was associated in Column B:

COLUMN A	COLUMN B
1 Irving Thalberg	**a** Hammer
2 Carl Laemmle	**b** 20th Century-Fox
3 David O. Selznick	**c** American-International
4 Harry Cohn	**d** MGM
5 B. P. Schulberg	**e** RKO

6 Darryl F. Zanuck	**f** Magna
7 Samuel Z. Arkoff	**g** Columbia
8 D. W. Griffith	**h** Paramount
9 James Carreras	**i** Universal
10 Mike Todd	**j** United Artists

■ **274.** Orson Welles was given the directorial assignment on *Touch of Evil* only because Charlton Heston, who'd heard Welles's name mentioned vaguely in connection with the project, told the studio that he'd gladly act in anything directed by Welles. The studio, which had signed Welles strictly as an actor, didn't want to lose Heston, so Welles was reluctantly allowed to take the helm. True or false?

■ **275.** Though it's clearly not a literal remake of Akira Kurosawa's *Rashomon*, this late-fifties American musical, with its four different viewpoints of a single story, certainly does remind one of the Kurosawa classic. Name the film.

C R I T I C S   O N   F I L M

Identify the films and the directors being discussed:

■ **276.** André Bazin: "[The film] is a wild imbroglio, a farandole danced to a frenetic rhythm in the corridors of a château and ending with an absurd cadaver. ... Neither the public nor the majority of the critics in 1939 could recognize in [the film] the fullest most lucid expression of a moribund age. ... The photographic style which prefigured the famous depth of field, now returned from America via *Citizen Kane* and *The Best Years of Our Lives*, appeared at the time a droll but dubious curiosity.   . It is admired not only for the most advanced expression of prewar French realism but also for its prefiguration of the most original elements of the cinematographic evolution of the next fifteen years. This legacy has yet to be exhausted."

■ **277.** Pauline Kael: "Movies generally work you up to expect the sensual intensities, but here you may be pulled into high without warning. Violence erupts crazily, too, the way it does in life—so unexpectedly fast that you can't believe it, and over before you've been able to take it in. The whole movie has this effect: it psychs you up to accept everything it shows you. And since the story deepens as it goes along, by the end you're likely to be openmouthed, trying to rethink what you've seen. Though the street language and the operatic style may be too much for those with conventional tastes, if this picture isn't a runaway success the reason could be that it's so original that some people will be dumbfounded—too struck to respond. It's about American life here and now, and it doesn't look like an American movie, or feel like one. If it were subtitled, we could hail a new European or South American talent—a new Buñuel steeped in Verdi, perhaps—and go home easier at heart. Because what [the director], who is thirty, has done with the experience of growing up in New York City has a thicker-textured rot and violence than we have ever had in an American movie, and a riper sense of evil. . . . The zinger in the movie— and it's this, I think, that begins to come together in one's head when the picture is over—is the way it gets at the psychological connections between Italian Catholicism and crime, between sin and crime."

■ **278.** Andrew Sarris: "[The film] is, in my unhumble opinion, the greatest film of all time, and I am willing to stake my critical reputation, such as it is, on this one proposition above all others. . . . Thus spake Sarris in the *Village Voice* in 1963. . . . After fifteen viewings, [the film] has yielded up to me not only its deepest beauties but also its most distracting faults. I fully understand why most other viewers can never love [the film] as devotedly as I do. To be moved by [the film] is to feel the emotion in motion itself as an expression of a director's delirium, and this is not an easy task for the conceptualized vision of the average viewer, conditioned for years to frame-by-frame pictorialism by which every shot is milked for all it's worth. What makes [this film] even more difficult to appreciate is its refusal to conform to the standard look of what most people tend to demand of a great film. [The film] sins first and foremost by being photographed in garish color rather than virtuous black-and-white and across a screen more wide than square. It is romantic rather than realistic, sensuous rather than severe. It glories less in the simplification of its style than in its elaboration as it glides and strides and turns and tracks across a fluid screen in the most dazzling display of baroque camera movement in the history of cinema. . . . It will all end in a New Orleans circus with [the heroine] selling for one dollar her presence to the multitudes, redeeming all men both as a woman and as an artistic reflection of their sensibilities, expressing in one long receding shot the cumulative explosion of the Romantic ego for the past two centuries. . . . I suppose I love [the film] because it transforms cinematic expression into a religious experience for this age of increasing faithlessness and fragmentation."

■ **279.** Jean Douchet: "[The first film] developed the vision of Death almost invincible and triumphant. Nothing really in the film can stop it. [The second film] seems to resume this pessimistic idea. There is however a fundamental difference between these two films. The Day practically doesn't exist in [the first film], only the idea of the Day. The world of the living was already offered to the Vampire. On the contrary, in [the second film], the Day is omnipresent throughout the film. Death is no longer a pure negation. [The director] sees it for what it really is: a necessity of life, without which life couldn't exist."

■ **280.** Donald Richie: "[The director's] last film, this is also his simplest. The ingredients are familiar; the colors are subdued; the viewing angle is invariable. Nothing is wanting, nothing is extraneous. At the same time there is an extraordinary intensification of mood in this picture. It is autumn again, but now it is deep autumn. Winter was always near, but now it will be tomorrow. At the same time, [the director's] regard was never kinder, never wiser. There is a mellowness about this picture which is stronger than nostalgia."

☆ ☆ ☆

■ **281.** Match the books in Column A with the films in which an actor or actress is seen reading them in Column B:

COLUMN A	COLUMN B
1 *Fritz Lang*	**a** *Reds*
2 Grace Metalious's *Peyton Place*	**b** François Truffaut's *Fahrenheit 451*
3 Charles Dickens's *David Copperfield*	**c** Herschell Gordon Lewis's *Blood Feast*
4 *Sexual Aberrations of the Criminal Female*	**d** Jean-Luc Godard's *Breathless* and Jim McBride's *Breathless*
5 William Shakespeare's *Othello*	**e** Jean-Luc Godard's *Contempt*
6 Holly Martins's *Oklahoma Kid*	**f** George Cukor's *A Double Life*
7 William Faulkner's *The Wild Palms*	**g** Frank Tashlin's *Will Success Spoil Rock Hunter?*
8 *Ancient Weird Religious Rites*	**h** Alfred Hitchcock's *Marnie*

■ **282.** This movie boasts one of the great plots in *noir* history: an innocent man, given a slow-acting poison for which there's no cure, attempts to find out who murdered him—and why—before he dies. Name the picture and its star.

■ **283.** Match the film in Column A with its ostensible biographical subject in Column B:

COLUMN A	COLUMN B
1 Robert Wise's *Star*	**a** Lillian Roth
2 Melville Shavelson's *Beau James*	**b** Jim Corbett
3 Charles Vidor's *Song Without End*	**c** Sigmund Romberg

4 Stanley Donen's *Deep in My*   **d** Lon Chaney
   Heart
5 Daniel Mann's *I'll Cry*   **e** Gertrude Lawrence
   Tomorrow
6 Raoul Walsh's *Gentleman Jim*   **f** Jimmy Walker
7 Joseph Pevney's *Man of a*   **g** Franz Liszt
   Thousand Faces
8 Fred F. Sear's *Cell 2455,*   **h** Caryl Chessman
   Death Row

■ **284.** Name the war movie in which Bill Mauldin, who rose to fame as a World War II cartoonist (he created Willie and Joe), very impressively played a major role.

■ **285.** Throughout much of the forties and early fifties, Howard Hawks tried to get Ernest Hemingway's *The Sun Also Rises* on the screen. One major problem, obviously, was the strict Production Code. In 1944, Hawks bought the rights to Sam Fuller's mystery novel, *The Dark Page*, and, a year later, let Fuller (not yet a director) take a crack at adapting *The Sun Also Rises*. In Fuller's first scene, Jake Barnes, a soldier wounded in action, is being operated on by a military doctor. Brett Ashley, a nurse, is there when Barnes's balls are dropped into a bucket! A quick, efficient, and outrageous writing stroke to clarify their later relationship. Needless to say, Fuller, too, was dropped. Hawks announced various actors for *The Sun Also Rises*— the most intriguing: Montgomery Clift as Jake Barnes, Gene Tierney as Brett Ashley, Dewey Martin as the matador—but he was never able to make the movie. In 1952, *The Dark Page* (which was once to have starred Humphrey Bogart and Lauren Bacall) was directed by Phil Karlson. It was called *Scandal Sheet* and starred Broderick Crawford, Donna Reed, and John Derek. True or false?

P O S T E R   A D   L I N E S

Name the films being advertised:

■ **286.** "A Mother. A Daughter. A Lover. Relationships can be murder."

■ **287.** "Four perfect killers. One perfect crime. Now all they have to fear is each other."

■ **288.** "It's a hot summer. Ned Racine is waiting for something special to happen. And when it does ... he won't be ready for the consequences. As the temperature rises, the suspense begins."

■ **289.** "One vicious hitman. One fierce cop. Ten thousand bullets."

■ **290.** "The celebrated story of a man obsessed by ideal beauty."

■ **291.** "Gambler. Junkie. Killer. Cop."

■ **292.** "A delightfully daring plan to give marriage a surprise ending."

■ **293.** "She knows all about love potions ... and lovely motions."

■ **294.** " 'You're no good and neither am I. We deserve each other!' "

■ **295.** "19 years old and married ... but not really."

QUIZ FOUR
★ ★ ★

Name the films in which the following lines appear as well as the actors who spoke them:

■ **296.** "The perfect woman would have the boobs of Elizabeth Taylor, the legs of Cyd Charisse, the wiggle of Monroe—and the smile of Michel Simon."

■ **297.** "This is funny. They calculated that between the first and the second man, four minutes must have passed. I mean, you throw a gangster off a train going eighty miles an hour and then you throw a second one, how much time passes between the two events, if the train doesn't change speed in between? Right? Four minutes."

■ **298.** ANNIE LAURIE STARR: "So what else do you like to do but shoot?"

BART: "That's been enough so far."

■ **299.** "*La revolución* is like a great love affair. In the beginning, she is a goddess, a holy cause. But every love affair has a terrible enemy—time. We see her as she is. *La revolución* is not a goddess but a

75

whore. She was never pure, never saintly, never perfect, and we run away, find another lover, another cause. Quick, sordid affairs—lust but no love, passion but no compassion. Without love, without a cause, we are nothing. We stay because we believe, we leave because we are disillusioned, we come back because we are lost, we die because we are committed."

■ **300.** "Aren't there any more comfortable men in this world? Now they're all little and nervous like sparrows or big and worried like sick bears. Men! ... If I ever loved a man again, I'd bear anything. He could have my teeth for watch fobs."

☆ ☆ ☆

■ **301.** Who nicknamed Joseph Francis Keaton "Buster"?

■ **302.** Match the directors in Column A and the cinematographers with whom they often worked in Column B:

COLUMN A	COLUMN B
1 Charlie Chaplin	**a** Elgin Lessley
2 Buster Keaton	**b** Bruce Surtees
3 Carol Reed	**c** Roland Totheroh
4 D. W. Griffith	**d** Russell Metty
5 Clint Eastwood	**e** Lucien Ballard
6 Budd Boetticher	**f** Billy Bitzer
7 Erick von Stroheim	**g** Joseph Biroc
8 Douglas Sirk	**h** William Daniels
9 Robert Aldrich	**i** Robert Krasker

■ **303.** Arthur Penn's *The Left-Handed Gun*, with Paul Newman as Billy the Kid, was based on a teleplay by that authentic voice of the American West, Gore Vidal. True or false?

■ **304.** Match the actors or actresses and films in Column
A with the original choices for the roles in Column
B:

COLUMN A   COLUMN B

1 Farley Granger in Alfred   **a** John Garfield
Hitchcock's *Strangers on
a Train*

2 Orson Welles in Carol Reed's   **b** Ronald Colman
The Third Man

3 Claude Rains in Alfred   **c** William Holden
Hitchcock's *Notorious*

4 Eva Marie Saint in Elia Kazan's   **d** George Raft
On the Waterfront

5 Jimmy Stewart in Alfred   **e** Clifton Webb
Hitchcock's *Rope*

6 Dick Powell in Edward   **f** Gary Cooper
Dmytryk's *Murder, My Sweet*

7 Gregory Peck in Alfred   **g** Grace Kelly
Hitchcock's *The Paradine Case*

8 Humphrey Bogart in John   **h** Noel Coward
Huston's *The Maltese Falcon*

9 Kim Novak in   **i** Burt Lancaster
Alfred Hitchcock's *Vertigo*

10 Clint Eastwood in Don Siegel's   **j** Cary Grant
Dirty Harry

11 Joseph Cotten in Alfred   **k** Vera Miles
Hitchcock's *Under Capricorn*

12 Joel McCrea in Alfred   **l** Paul Newman
Hitchcock's *Foreign
Correspondent*

■ **305.** In Orson Welles's opinion, "the greatest actor who
ever lived" was (a) Charlie Chaplin (b) John Barrymore (c) George Arliss (d) Raimu (e) John Gielgud?

C R I T I C S   O N   F I L M

Identify the films and the directors being discussed:

■ **306.** James Agee: "[The film.] I see no signs of originality in [the director's] work; a sickening lack of mental firmness, of fundamental moral aliveness, and of taste; but at his best an extremely vigorous talent for improvisation, for naturalistic poetry, and for giving the illusion of the present tense. He is the best of the few good improvisers at work. The best of this movie is the best that has come out of Italy; highly gratifying and exciting; the worst is sycophantic, vulgar, lick-spittle stuff which could begin to be forgivable only in a man of, say, D. W. Griffith's size.

■ **307.** Peter Bogdanovich: "[The film] tells a ridiculously simple and unassuming story of one fairly insignificant man's life—from birth to death—which [the director] turns into a moving testament to the inherent beauty behind our daily frivolousness and vanity, our petty crises, our indiscretions, our deepest vulnerability. It is [the director's] 'divine comedy,' and no one has ever been more gentle or bemused by the weaknesses of humanity. When the hero of the picture dies behind (of course) a closed door, [the director's] camera slowly retreats to take in a ballroom, and an old waltz the man loved begins to play, and death has no dominion. No other image I can think of more aptly or more movingly conveys [the director's] generosity or tolerance: the man has died—long live man."

■ **308.** François Truffaut: "The opening credits unfold during a train holdup on the Mexican border. One of the two bandits dies in the arms of his accomplice, Santiago, who wanders around all night until he meets a young farmer, Manuel, and his charming wife, Maria. The film tells the story of Santiago and Manuel's trip to the city to sell the watches Santiago has stolen, their stopover in a cabaret on the way home, and an explosive and unexpected finale. What counts are the delicate and ambiguous relationships among the three, the stuff of a good novel. One of the most beautiful modern novels I know is *Jules and Jim* by Henri-Pierre Roché, which shows how, over a lifetime, two friends and the woman companion they share love one another with tenderness and almost no harshness, thanks to an esthetic morality constantly reconsidered. [The film] is the first film that has made me think that *Jules and Jim* could be done as a film."

■ **309.** Robert Benayoun: "One can see that in [the film], [the director] has ended up by shooting just the kind of film he would once have attacked: the very principle of a commentary lifted straight from the book ... and read, quite simply, on the soundtrack, contradicts all that [the director] was foolish enough one day to write. By this I mean that [the director], whose lack of culture has always astonished me, had a lot of luck to come across a good book, to have liked and understood it."

■ **310.** James Agee: "Apparently [the film], which I must say I liked, is working up a rather serious reputation as a fine melodrama. Why? It is obviously an improvement on one of the world's worst plays; but it is not such an improvement that that is not

obvious. ... [The director] still has a twenties director's correct feeling that everything, including
the camera, should move; but the camera should
move for purposes other than those of a nautch-
dancer, and the bit players and atmospheric scenes
are not even alien corn.   [The film] is   rever-
ently spoken of as (1) fuñ, (2) a 'real movie.' I still
think it is the year's clearest measure of how will-
ingly, *faute de mieux*, people will deceive themselves. Even *Jeannie* [directed by Harold French],
hardly a movie at all, was better fun; or even that
affable imitation-of-an-imitation, *Tartu* [directed by
Harold S. Bucquet]."

☆ ☆ ☆

■ **311.** Match the books in Column A with the films in
which an actor or actress is seen reading them in
Column B:

COLUMN A

1 Willa Cather's *My
Ántonia*

2 Irving Shulman's *Cry
Tough*
3 Raymond Chandler's
The Big Sleep
4 *Japanese Women*

5 F. Scott Fitzgerald's
Tender Is the Night

6 William Shakespeare's
Hamlet
7 Mikhael Bakunin's *The
Patriotism*

COLUMN B

a Martin Scorsese's *Who's
That Knocking at My
Door*
b Lindsay Anderson's
This Sporting Life
c Robert Bresson's *Une
Femme douce*
d Douglas Sirk's *The
Tarnished Angels*
e Michael Powell's and
Emeric Pressburger's
The Wild Heart
f Jean-Luc Godard's
Alphaville
g François Truffaut's
Shoot the Piano Player

8 Alexander Alekhine's *My Best Games of Chess*

9 *Spells and Charms of Mary Woodus*

10 *La Timidité*

h Sergio Leone's *Duck, You Sucker!* (a.k.a. *A Fistful of Dynamite*)

i François Truffaut's *Bed and Board*

j Michael Powell's and Emeric Pressburger's *Stairway to Heaven*

■ **312.** Federico Fellini, Roger Vadim, and Louis Malle each directed one segment of *Spirits of the Dead*, a 1969 anthology film. Fellini accepted the assignment only after being assured that the other directors, whom Vadim and Malle eventually replaced, would be two of the best directors in the world. Fellini was mortified when they dropped out. Name them.

■ **313.** Match the film in Column A with its ostensible biographical subject in Column B:

Column A

1 Preston Sturges's *The Great Moment*

2 Norman Jewison's *Gaily, Gaily*

3 Art Napoleon's *Too Much, Too Soon*

4 John Ford's *The Long Gray Line*

5 John Frankenheimer's *Birdman of Alcatraz*

6 John Boulting's *The Magic Box*

7 Alfred Hitchcock's *The Wrong Man*

8 John Ford's *The Wings of Eagles*

Column B

a William Friese-Greene

b Martin Maher

c William T. G. Morton

d Frank "Spig" Wead

e Manny Balestrero

f Diana Barrymore

g Robert Stroud

h Ben Hecht

314. In Clint Eastwood's fourth major movie as an actor—after Sergio Leone's *A Fistful of Dollars, For a Few Dollars More,* and *The Good the Bad and the Ugly*—he was directed by Vittorio De Sica. True or false?

315. Name the director who said, "The picture was so bad they had to do retakes before it could be put on the shelf."

P O S T E R   A D   L I N E S

Name the films being advertised:

316. "On every street in every city in this country there's a nobody who dreams of being a somebody."

317. "Revolvers bark! Figures steal slowly among the shadows of the night! Then all is still . . ."

318. "Crushed lips don't talk!"

319. "There never was a man like . . . There never was a picture like . "

320. "The world's most beautiful animal."

321. "There's nothing sweeter than revenge."

322. "Ogata supports his wife, his lover, the local yakuza gang, the family barbershop, and a mystical carp by making 8mm porno films."

323. "A crazy surreal comedy on the history of human folly."

324. "Three Men With Dreams! One Woman With a Plan! There is no such thing as simple Love."

325. "Is Kitty a mother?"

■ **326.** "I used to be somebody else, but I traded myself in ..."

■ **327.** "The thousands who have read the book will know why WE WILL NOT SELL ANY CHILDREN TICKETS to see this picture."

■ **328.** "When there's no more room in Hell, the dead will walk the earth ..."

■ **329.** "It's tremonstrous!"

■ **330.** " 'You're no blue-blood any more, honey. The master bought you ... and now he's waitin'!' "

QUIZ FIVE

Name the films in which these memorable opening lines appear and in some cases the actors who spoke them:

■ **331.** "Venice. Spring 1866. The last months of the Austrian occupation of the Venetian provinces. The Italian government has concluded an alliance with Prussia and the war of Liberation is imminent."

■ **332.** "I never knew the old Vienna before the war, with its Strauss music, its glamour, and its easy charm. I really got to know it in the classic period of the black market."

■ **333.** "One funeral is just like another but this one is special: not one man. Only women, nothing but women. Bertrand would have enjoyed the sight of his own funeral."

■ **334.** "Who am I in this story? ... The author? The announcer? A passerby? I am you. In fact, anyone among you. I am the personification of your desire, of your desire to know everything. People always know only one side of reality. And why? Be-

84

cause they see only one side of things. But I . . . I 'see' from every side. That allows me to be everywhere at the same time. Everywhere! But where are we? On a stage? In a studio? It is hard to say. . . . Oh! We are in Vienna. In 1900. . . . We are in the past. I adore the past. It is so much more restful than the present and so much more reliable than the future. The sun's out, and it's spring! The fragrance in the air tells you that this is going to be a story about love. What do we need for love to begin its merry-go-round? A waltz. There! A waltz!"

■ **335.** "I suppose that when you spend most of your life in one profession, you develop what could be called an occupational point of view. So maybe I can be forgiven for the first thing I thought of that morning. Because I found myself thinking that the staging and setting, even the lighting, of Maria's funeral were just what she would have wanted. My name is . . . I've been a writer and director of movies for longer than I like to remember. I go way back, back to when the movies had two dimensions, and one dimension and sometimes no dimension at all."

☆ ☆ ☆

■ **336.** George Jessel wrote this poem from the p.o.v. of his actress wife, about her and her sister. Name them.

> *The Vitagraph Picture Studios*
> *Were in our neighborhood.*
> *And I started appearing on the screen*
> *When I was fourteen.*

At sixteen
I was the leading woman
In the biggest epic of that time:
The Battle-Cry of Peace.
And I brought my sister Constance
Into the movies, too.
She was as blonde
As I was dark,
And we both became stars.
Lewis J. Selznick,
The first of the great movie showmen,
Printed our names
On the top of tall buildings
Everywhere.

■ **337.** Robert Benayoun, criticizing a specific film movement, wrote: "If the cinema looks in upon itself too much . . . it will be as though it were shut up in a furnished apartment whose walls were covered with photographs of furniture, whose only books were about furnishing." These directors, he went on, made films in which "such and such a scene from Hitchcock coupled with another one from Buñuel, leads up to a long Vigo sequence, shot in a Rossellini manner, but rejuvenated by Chayefsky techniques." François Giroud, writing in *L'Express* about Marcel Carné's *Les Tricheurs*, coined the term for this movement, which was in open revolt against films such as Carné's. Name it.

■ **338.** In Hollywood, he was called "the boy wonder" and would become the protagonist of F. Scott Fitzgerald's *The Last Tycoon* (as production executive Monroe Stahr). He was married to one of MGM's top stars. When their first child, a son, was born, Eddie Cantor wired them: "Congratulations on your latest production. Am sure it will look better after it's been cut." He died at the age of thirty-seven, after which his wife began making career mistakes (e.g., turning down a starring role in *Gone With the Wind*.) Name the couple.

■ **339.** What famous novelist, usually associated with Howard Hawks, worked uncredited on John Ford's *Drums Along the Mohawk* and Jean Renoir's *The Southerner*?

■ **340.** In what movie does Barbra Streisand play a Communist?

D I R E C T O R S   O N   F I L M
Identify the directors doing the talking:

■ **341.** "The film is like a battleground. Love. Hate. Action. Violence. Death. In one word: emotion."

■ **342.** "I always think of my style as a curious cross between Lubitsch and Stroheim.   . I'm not an outdoor man. I've never done a Western. I think I should confine myself to bedrooms maybe. I was saying to Willie Wyler the other day: 'I'm doing a picture where the boss is chasing a secretary around a desk. But I'm no fool. I'm going to have Andrew Marton shoot the chase sequence.' "

■ **343.** "My parents spoke of *piety*, of *love*, and of *humility*. I have really tried hard. But as long as there was a God in my world, I couldn't even get close to my goals. My humility was not humble enough. My love remained nonetheless far less than the love of Christ or of the saints or even my own mother's love. And my piety was forever poisoned by grave doubts. Now that God is gone, I feel that *all this* is mine: *piety* towards life, *humility* before my meaningless fate, and *love* for the other children who are afraid, who are ill, who are cruel."

■ **344.** "I think my appreciation for the horizontal line came through my association with Frank Lloyd Wright, and I like to compose within a horizontal frame."

■ **345.** "I'm not against the police. I'm just afraid of them."

☆ ☆ ☆

■ **346.** SIGNS IN THE CINEMA. Match the sign in Column A with the film in which it appears in Column B:

COLUMN A	COLUMN B
1 WHAT IS TRUTH	**a** Francis Coppola's *Apocalypse Now*
2 THEY CAN HAVE MY GUN WHEN THEY PRY IT FROM MY COLD DEAD FINGERS	**b** Joseph L. Mankiewicz's *Guys and Dolls*
3 THE WORLD IS YOURS	**c** George Cukor's *Les Girls*
4 DEATH FROM ABOVE	**d** John Milius's *Red Dawn*
5 SAVE A SOUL MISSION	**e** Alfred Hitchcock's *Psycho*
6 BATES MOTEL	**f** Howard Hawks's *Scarface* and Brian De Palma's *Scarface*

■ **347.** Pope Piux XII considered excommunicating this director for the film he had made. The director said of his film: "I tried to portray a society that no longer has any passions, any guts. What *has* it got? Conventions, clothes, attitudes, smiles, horn-rimmed spectacles, feathers, chairs, tapestries.   " Name the film and its director

■ **348.** This famous British novelist was once a movie critic and caused a scandal when he reviewed John Ford's *Wee Willie Winkie* The film's child star, Shirley Temple, he wrote, was a "complete totsy" whose "well-developed rump" was "as voluptuous in gray flannel trousers as Miss Dietrich's," arousing her audience of "middle-aged men and clergymen " Name this novelist/critic

■ **349.** He was an extra in silent pictures, then worked his way up. In the thirties and forties, he starred in films directed by Howard Hawks, Alfred Hitchcock, Preston Sturges, and George Stevens. After 1946, in an odd career turn, he mostly played cowboys. In 1962, at the age of fifty-seven, he made his most memorable Western. Name the actor and the movie.

■ **350.** In what film does Alfred Hitchcock delude both the picture's heroine and the audience by presenting a murderer's deliberate lie (he claims he was framed) as the truth? As a result, many of the film's flashbacks falsify what really happened.

L A S T L I N E S

Name the films in which these memorable closing lines appear as well as the actors who spoke them:

■ **351.** "There is no emperor. There is only an empress."

■ **352.** "Just say I'm old-fashioned. That should be enough."

■ **353.** "The horror. The horror."

■ **354.** "He thought that in quantities he might find happiness. Is it necessary to go through an endless quest for what we're told can be found in one person? In any case, something will endure of the women he loved—a token of remembrance, a rectangular object, 325 bound pages: a book."

■ **355.** [Sings] "Falling in love again. Never wanted to. What am I to do? Can't help it!"

QUIZ FIVE
☆ ☆

Name the films in which these memorable opening lines appear and in some cases the actors who spoke them:

■ **356.** "Well, then, now, I'll begin at the beginning. A fine, soft day in the spring it was when the train pulled into Castletown, three hours late as usual, and himself got off. He didn't have the look of an American tourist at all about him. Not a camera on him and, what was worse, not even a fishing rod."

■ **357.** "This play, a fantasy in the Italian style, takes place at the beginning of the Eighteenth Century in a Spanish colony in South America. Within these territories, which were governed by viceroys appointed by his most Catholic majesty, the King of Spain, the predominant influence was that of the Church. On occasion, troupes of Italian actors crossed to the New World to seek their fortune, driven by hardship and a vision."

■ **358.** "Come on in! Come and have a look at her. Come and see Truth herself! Come on in. Don't just stand there because once you've seen Truth herself, you'll think of her by day and you'll dream of her by night. Just have one look at her. She's wearing the simplest of garments—she's dressed in nothing but her beauty, she shows herself unveiled to all of you. Come on in. Pay on the way out. Don't let this unique experience pass you by. Gentlemen, you'll never forgive yourself if you miss this vision of delight. Voluptuous, daring, enough to make you tremble with desire. A show for those who don't keep their eyes in their pockets. No children allowed."

■ **359.** "On November first, 1959, the population of New York City was 8,042,783. If you laid all these people end to end, figuring an average height of five feet six and a half inches, they would reach from Times Square to Karachi, Pakistan. I know facts like this because I work for an insurance company."

■ **360.** "This story begins between night and day, at the crack of dawn. Monmartre is between heaven and ... hell."

☆ ☆ ☆

■ **361.** Andrew Sarris, talking about a particular fifties film, called its stars "the most beautiful couple in the history of the cinema. It was a sensuous experience to watch them respond to each other. Those gigantic close-ups of them kissing were unnerving—sybaritic—like gorging on chocolate sundaes." Sarris had in mind (a) Montgomery Clift and Elizabeth Taylor in George Stevens's *A Place in the Sun* (b) Charlie Chaplin and Claire Bloom in Chaplin's *Limelight* (c) John Wayne and Maureen

O'Hara in John Ford's *The Quiet Man* (d) Sterling Hayden and Joan Crawford in Nicholas Ray's *Johnny Guitar* (e) Cary Grant and Grace Kelly in Alfred Hitchcock's *To Catch a Thief*?

■ **362.** His father was an anarchist executed during World War I by the Clemenceau government. The director's most famous film was banned in his own country for more than ten years by the official film censor. Name the director and the picture.

■ **363.** Match the films in Column A with the novels on which they were based in Column B:

COLUMN A	COLUMN B
1 Jacques Tourneur's *Out of the Past*	**a** Whit Masterson's *Badge of Evil*
2 John Brahm's *The Brasher Doubloon*	**b** Richard Stark's *The Hunter*
3 François Truffaut's *Shoot the Piano Player*	**c** Raymond Chandler's *The Little Sister*
4 John Boorman's *Point Blank*	**d** Ira Wolfert's *Tucker's People*
5 Allan Dwan's *Slightly Scarlet*	**e** Geoffrey Homes's *Build My Gallows High*
6 Alfred Hitchcock's *Secret Agent*	**f** Joseph Conrad's *The Secret Agent*
7 Orson Welles's *Touch of Evil*	**g** Robert L. Pike's *Mute Witness*
8 Alfred Hitchcock's *Vertigo*	**h** Raymond Chandler's *The High Window*
9 Robert Aldrich's *The Grissom Gang*	**i** James M. Cain's *Love's Lovely Counterfeit*
10 Abraham Polonsky's *Force of Evil*	**j** Francis Iles's *Before the Fact*

11 Alfred Hitchcock's
Spellbound

k James Hadley Chase's
*No Orchids for Miss
Blandish*

12 Paul Bogart's *Marlowe*

l Pierre Boileau's and
Thomas Narcejac's
D'Entre les morts

13 Alfred Hitchcock's
Suspicion

m W. Somerset
Maugham's *Ashenden*

14 Peter Yates's *Bullitt*

n David Goodis's *Down
There*

15 Alfred Hitchcock's
Sabotage

o Francis Beeding's *The
House of Dr. Edwardes*

■ **364.** In a film that he directed—based on a story by Orson Welles—Charlie Chaplin played a serial killer. True or false?

■ **365.** He spent the latter part of the thirties in Mexico learning to be a matador. In 1941, he was hired as a technical adviser on Rouben Mamoulian's *Blood and Sand*. He began directing in 1944, but his early movies didn't amount to much. In 1951, with the help of John Wayne (who produced) and John Ford (who assisted in the editing), he made what he considered his first real film, a superb, largely autobiographical work that failed commercially but established him—at least to those who really love films—as an outstanding director. Name the picture and its director.

DIRECTORS ON FILM
Identify the directors doing the talking:

■ **366.** "This picture—I don't give a fuck what anyone says. If you don't have time to see it, don't. If you don't like it, don't. If it doesn't give you answer, fuck you. I didn't make it for you anyway."

■ **367.** "The motion picture is softening the hard life of the plain citizen with beauty and sweetness; it keeps men away from the saloons and drink, because it gives them a place of recreation in pleasant surroundings; it brings to the poor who are unable to travel away from their own dingy surroundings the beauty and poetry of moving foreign scenes, of flowers, waving grasses, the beauty of uplifted mountain crests, and the wonders of nature."

■ **368.** "I'd like to be able to make a Western like Kurosawa makes Westerns."

■ **369.** "In [the film], I was not able to achieve more than sixty percent of what the script demanded. There were many reasons for this, one of them a peculiarly technical one. An Arriflex had just come and it jammed frequently during the shooting in Benares. It became impossible to do more than one take of a scene. Another problem was that Ravi Shankar should have composed half as much more music than he did. But I find the psychological aspect—the relationship between a growing Apu and his mother—very successful."

■ **370.** "I have been ruined by lack of money. All my good films, which I financed myself, made nothing. Only my bad films made money. Money has been my ruin. . . . Unfortunately, the public is not convinced when the lovers are not handsome."

☆ ☆ ☆

■ **371.** SIGNS IN THE CINEMA. Match the sign in Column A with the film in which it appears in Column B:

Column A	Column B
1 HMS JONAH	**a** Elia Kazan's *A Face in the Crowd*
2 MATUSCHEK & CO	**b** Joseph L. Mankiewicz's *The Barefoot Contessa*
3 FIGHTERS FOR FULLER	**c** Ernst Lubitsch's *The Shop Around the Corner*
4 HOSPITAL MANULANI	**d** Sergio Leone's *Once Upon a Time in the West*
5 CHE SERA SERA	**e** Billy Wilder's *The Private Life of Sherlock Holmes*
6 STATION	**f** John Ford's *Donovan's Reef*

■ **372.** Italy's huge studio complex, Cinecittà was built (a) in 1922 at the height of the Italian silent film (b) immediately after World War II to train the new generation of directors: Roberto Rossellini, Federico Fellini, Luchino Visconti, et al. (c) by order of Mussolini in 1935 to propagate the glory of the fascist regime (d) in 1955 to churn out television fodder for the growing European market (e) in the early sixties to handle the swelling number of Italian productions, especially spaghetti Westerns and costume dramas?

■ **373.** Match the director in Column A with the novel he wrote in Column B:

Column A	Column B
1 Tay Garnett	**a** *A Man Laughs Back*
2 Richard Brooks	**b** *The Arrangement*
3 Erich von Stroheim	**c** *One for the Book*
4 Michael Powell	**d** *Mr. Arkadin*
5 Edmund Goulding	**e** *Killing a Mouse on Sunday*
6 Orson Welles	**f** *A Waiting Game*

7	Jean Renoir	**g**	*The Ragazzr*
8	Sam Fuller	**h**	*The Unaltered Cat*
9	Albert Lewin	**i**	*The Notebooks of Captain Georges*
10	Elia Kazan	**j**	*Burn, Baby, Burn!*
11	Pier Paolo Pasolini	**k**	*Paprika*
12	Emeric Pressburger	**l**	*The Brick Foxhole*

■ **374.** A staircase appears in the first scene of Mark Robson's and Val Lewton's *The Seventh Victim*. It was built for another film, a famous one in which the camera ascends alongside the huge Victorian stairs as Tim Holt follows Agnes Moorehead to the top. Name the film and the director.

■ **375.** Name the notoriously foulmouthed studio head who pontificated, "Lemme tell you what this business is all about. It's cunt and horses!"

L · A · S · T · · · L · I · N · E · S

Name the films in which these memorable closing lines appear and in some cases the actors who spoke them:

■ **376.** "What does *degueulasse* mean?"

■ **377.** CHORUS OF SHOUTS (OFF-CAMERA): "Death to the bourgeoisie!"

FEMALE VOICE-OVER: "To dare to rebel. For us, this means fighting here and now on two fronts, against the bourgeoisie and its ally, revisionism."

TITLE (BLACK AND RED LETTERS): THERE ARE IN THE WORLD TODAY TWO WINDS—THE EAST WIND AND THE WEST WIND. THE

EAST WIND ACTUALLY PREVAILS
OVER THE WEST WIND. THE
REVOLUTIONARY FORCES HAVE
ACHIEVED AN OVERWHELMING
SUPERIORITY OVER THE
IMPERIALIST FORCES."

■ **378.** "Positively the same dame."

■ **379.** "Oh, if only you could have recognized what was always yours, we could have found what was never lost."

■ **380.** "It's not difficult to die. The difficult thing is to live. [sound of a firing squad] God forgive them, for they know not what they do."

QUIZ FIVE
★ ★ ★

Name the films in which these memorable opening lines appear and in some cases the actors who spoke them:

■ **381.** [Sings] "The mystery of night ... has stolen the light...."

■ **382.** "When the child was a child it walked with its arms swinging. It wanted the stream to be a river, the river a torrent, this puddle to be the sea. When the child was a child, it didn't know it was a child. Everything was full of life and all life was one. When the child was a child, it had no opinions about anything. It had no habits. It sat cross-legged, took off running, and didn't make a face when photographed."

■ **383.** "Once a day is plenty. Just a couple of flies, a sip of milk and perhaps a pigeon's egg on Sundays."

■ **384.** "This is the door of scares. It's just an ordinary door—wood, painted red—but behind this door is death."

99

■ **385.** "To conquer the world Francis became humble so as to be worthy of the kingdom of heaven. Everyone mocked him and said he was mad. But Pope Innocent III let him preach to the people."

☆ ☆ ☆

■ **386.** Name the well-known actor who once went six rounds with heavyweight champion Jack Johnson and who served as provost marshal of Baghdad.

■ **387.** From the early twenties to the end of World War II, the Japanese film industry produced over 10,000 films. By war's end, what number had survived? (a) 1,200 (b) over 8,000 (c) none (d) less than forty (e) 5,632.

■ **388.** Match the films in Column A with the novels on which they were based in Column B:

COLUMN A

1 François Truffaut's *Mississippi Mermaid*
2 Hobart Henley's *Roadhouse Nights*
3 Fritz Lang's *The Woman in the Window*
4 Jean-Luc Godard's *Band of Outsiders*
5 Stanley Kubrick's *The Killing*
6 Orson Welles's *The Lady From Shangai*

7 Claude Chabrol's *A Double Take* (a.k.a. *Leda* and *Web of Passion*)

COLUMN B

a Charles Einstein's *The Bloody Spur*
b Anthony Gilbert's *The Woman in Red*
c Lionel White's *Clean Break*
d Richard Murphy's *The Chair for Martin Rome*
e William Irish's *Waltz Into Darkness*
f Arthur LaBern's *Goodbye Piccadilly, Farewell Leicester Square*
g Dolores Hitchens's *Fool's Gold*

8 Alfred Hitchcock's
  Frenzy
9 Fritz Lang's *While
  the City Sleeps*
10 Alfred Hitchcock's
  The Lady Vanishes
11 Joseph L. Mankiewicz's
  House of Strangers
12 Joseph H. Lewis's
  My Name Is Julia Ross
13 Alfred Hitchcock's
  Family Plot
14 Robert Siodmak's *Cry
  of the City*

h J. H. Wallis's *Once Off
  Guard*
i Dashiell Hammett's
  Red Harvest
j Victor Canning's
  The Rainbird Pattern
k Jerome Weidman's *I'll
  Never Go There Again*
l Sherwood King's
  Before I Die
m Stanley Ellin's *The Key
  to Nicholas Street*
n Ethel Lina White's
  The Wheel Spins

■ **389.** They were both born Jimmy Stewart—the American actor in 1908, the English actor in 1913. Obviously, one Jimmy Stewart in movies was enough, so the younger man changed his name in the late thirties. Name the rechristened British actor.

■ **390.** In the late fifties, Jean-Luc Godard's choice for "the greatest title in all cinema, sound or silent" was (a) Max Ophuls's *Le Plaisir* (b) Frank Borzage's *History Is Made at Night* (c) D. W. Griffith's *True-Heart Susie* (d) Charlie Chaplin's *City Lights* (e) Orson Welles's *Chimes at Midnight* (f) Douglas Sirk's *A Time to Love and a Time to Die*? His choice for second-greatest title is also included in this list. Name that one, too.

DIRECTORS ON FILM

Identify the directors doing the talking:

■ **391.** "I'm not afraid of death. I'm afraid of dying alone in a hotel room, with my bags open and a shooting script on the night table I must know whose fingers will close my eyes."

■ **392.** "I always try to remain impassive. I think that the surprising, extraordinary, moving thing about men is just that the great actions and achievements occur in the same way as the ordinary acts involved in living; it is with the same humility that I try to translate one into the other; there lies a source of dramatic interest."

■ **393.** "Allowing others to prepare a scenario for a director is like giving a finished drawing to a painter and asking him to put in the colors."

■ **394.** "I really am looking for absolution for all the things I had to do for money's sake."

■ **395.** "As you get older, the far-off past becomes clearer. The recent past you can't remember as well."

☆ ☆ ☆

■ **396.** SIGNS IN THE CINEMA. Match the sign in Column A with the film in which it appears in Column B:

COLUMN A	COLUMN B
1 THIS GIRL IS NOT GUILTY WITH ME. WES MCQUEEN	**a** Edgar G. Ulmer's *Detour*
2 TO-NIGHT GOLDEN CURLS	**b** Frank Borzage's *Desire*
3 HICKORY WOOD FARM	**c** John Huston's *The Asphalt Jungle*
4 JEREMIAH PRODUCTIONS	**d** Alfred Hitchcock's *The Lodger*
5 ZELTON JEWELERS	**e** Jean-Luc Godard's *Contempt*
6 BREAK O'DAWN CLUB	**f** Raoul Walsh's *Colorado Territory*

7 I AM HAPPY TO DRIVE   **g** Nicholas Ray's *They*
  A BRONSON **8**   *Live by Night*

■ **397.** When Federico Fellini planned to make a film of *Don Quixote*, he asked comedy director/actor Jacques Tati to play the title role. True or false?

■ **398.** Alfred Hitchcock's *Rope* has gained considerable attention because, except for its opening shot (after which there is an undisguised cut), it was filmed in eight ten-minute takes and carefully designed— with the beginnings and ends of reels cleverly camouflaged—to look like one continuous shot. For what other film did Hitchcock want to use the same technique?

■ **399.** The screenplay was an "original," nevertheless it included bits and pieces taken from newspaper stories, from John Steinbeck's *The Moon Is Down*, and from Ferenc Molnar's *The Boys of Paul Street* (which Frank Borzage had made in Hollywood as *No Greater Glory* in 1934). Name the film.

■ **400.** What father and son, both Hollywood stars, each died on the set of a film—the father in 1931, the son in 1959? Name the pictures.

L A S T   L I N E S

Name the films in which these memorable closing lines appear and in some cases the actors who spoke them:

■ **401.** "Yes, Inger, I have found your faith. Now life is beginning for us."

■ **402.** "A lot of people loved my husband, but he never loved anyone. That's why he's dead."

■ **403.** "Instead of prison walls—bloom flowery fields."

■ **404.** " 'No beast so fierce but knows some touch of pity. But I know none, and therefore am no beast.' "

■ **405.** "I'm killing myself because you've never loved me, because I never loved you. I'm killing myself because our affair was so slipshod, in order to bind us together again. I'll leave an indelible mark on you."

PHOTO QUIZ

Q U E S T I O N S   4 0 6 – 4 3 5

Once a decade, beginning in the fifties, the British film magazine *Sight & Sound* has published a list of the Top Ten films of all time, based on a poll of critics from all over the world (*see* Quiz Two, questions 144–150 in the ✩✩✩ section). Since many of the films carry over from one list to the next, the total number of films from the five lists of Top Ten films is in fact only thirty. This Photo Quiz includes a still from each of these films, arranged in chronological order. Name them.

■ 406

■ 407

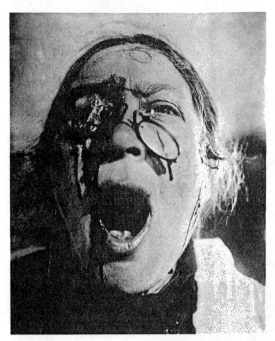

■ 408

■ 409

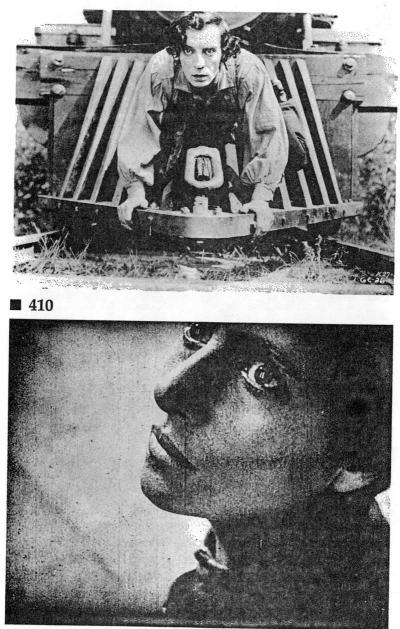

■ 410

■ 411

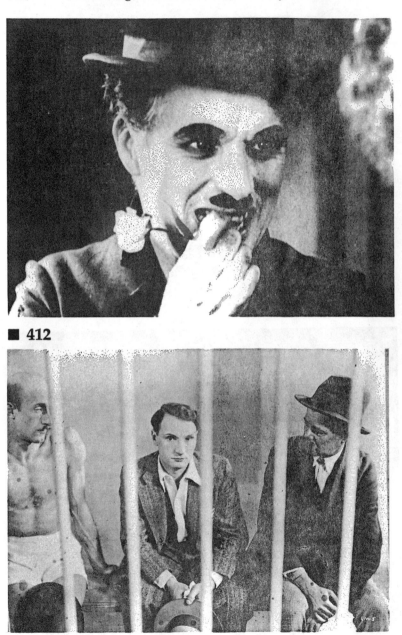

■ 412

■ 413

■ 414

■ 415

■ 416

■ 417

■ **418**

■ **419**

■ **420**

■ **421**

■ 422

■ 423

■ 424

■ 425

■ 426

■ 427

■ 428

■ 429

■ 430

■ 431

■ **432**

■ **433**

■ 434

■ 435

QUIZ SIX

M E M O R A B L E   L I N E S

Name the films in which the following lines appear as well as the actors who spoke them:

■ **436.** "We rob banks."

■ **437.** ACTOR: "Have you never in your life or travels had any encounter with, or experience of, what Larry the crackpot would describe as a love life?"

ACTRESS: "There are worse things than chastity, Mr. Shannon."

ACTOR: "Yes, lunacy and death."

ACTRESS: "... Yes, I have had two experiences, well, encounters. ... One evening ... I went out in the sampan with the Aussie underwear salesman. I noticed he became more and more agitated ... he looked intensely and passionately into my eyes and said, 'Would you do me a favor, would you do something for me?' 'What?' I asked. 'Well,' he said, 'if I turn my back, if I look the other way, will you take off some piece of your clothing and let me hold it, just hold it?' . . . I did as he asked and he kept his promise, he kept his back turned until I said 'Ready' and threw him the piece of clothing."

ACTOR: "But what did he do with it?"

ACTRESS: "I don't know, I looked the other way.'

ACTOR: "And that experience you call that a . .'

ACTRESS: "A love experience? Yes I do, Mr. Shannon."

■ **438.** "Come on, you never read an actuarial table in your life. I've got ten volumes on suicide alone. Suicide by race, by color, by occupation, by sex, by seasons of the year, by time of day. Suicide, how committed: by poisons, by firearms, by drowning, by leaps. Suicide by poison divided by types of poison, such as corrosive, irritant, systemic, gaseous, narcotic, alkaloid, protein and so forth. Suicide by leaps, subdivided by leaps from high places, under the wheels of trains, under the wheels of trucks, under the feet of horses, from steamboats. But, Mr. Norton, of all the cases on record, there's not one single case of suicide by leap from the rear end of a moving train."

■ **439.** "I promise you we'll blast hair all over them walls!"

■ **440.** "My mother thanks you, my father thanks you, my sister thanks you, and I thank you."

☆ ☆ ☆

■ **441.** The daughter of a Speaker of the House of Representatives, this stage and screen star was known for her wit and lack of inhibition. Hume Cronyn

remembered that, on the set of an Alfred Hitchcock film, the actress "somewhere along the way
got tired of wearing underwear. We all had to
climb up a ladder to get into the tank with the
boat, and there she was—exposed for all to see.
One day a lady from *Good Housekeeping* visited the
set and she was outraged. She went off to the
front office and raised absolute hell. . . . But Hitch
simply replied: 'In a case like this, it's hard to de-
cide where the responsibility lies. You might consider this a matter for the wardrobe department,
or perhaps for the makeup people—or perhaps
it's even for hairdressing.' " Name the actress and
the film.

■ **442.** John Ford's *The Searchers* (1956) is certainly among
the most praised of all American films—and
rightly so. Not many years after making it, Ford
returned to the theme of men who find and bring
back captive white children from the Indians. This
"sequel" to *The Searchers*, though not a great film,
is very good—and a fascinating companion piece
to the earlier picture. Yet it has been strangely and
unjustly neglected. Name the film.

■ **443.** The four movie artists who founded United Artists
were Mary Pickford, Douglas Fairbanks, Charlie
Chaplin, and (a) William S. Hart (b) Joseph
Schenck (c) D. W. Griffith (d) Fred Niblo
(e) Thomas Ince?

■ **444.** Joseph Goebbels, Nazi propaganda minister and
director of Germany's film industry, filed a suit for
copyright infringement against Charlie Chaplin,
claiming (with good reason) that Chaplin's *Modern
Times* plagiarized what film: (a) Jean Vigo's *Zéro de*

conduite (b) Jean Renoir's *La Chienne* (c) René Clair's *A nous la liberté* (d) Marcel Carné's *Le Jour se lève* (e) Jacques Feyder's *Crainquebille?*

■ **445.** A disgruntled French critic referred to this controversial theory as "a dialectic of hormonal rejuvenation." One of its principal defenders, Andrew Sarris, wrote: "The art of the cinema is the art of an attitude, the style of a gesture. It is not so much *what* as *how*. The *what* is some aspect of reality rendered mechanically by the camera. The *how* is what [some] French critics designate somewhat mystically as mise-en-scène. [The theory] criticism is a reaction against sociological criticism that enthroned the *what* against the *how*. However, it would be equally fallacious to enthrone the *how* into a personal statement. . . . The strong director imposes his own personality on a film: the weak director allows the personalities of others to run rampant. . . . Obviously, [the theory] cannot possibly cover every vagrant charm of the cinema. Nonetheless, the listing of films by directors remains the most reliable index of quality available to us short of the microscopic evaluation of every film ever made." Name the highly disputed theory.

A C T O R S   O N   F I L M

Identify the actors (and in one case the film) being discussed:

■ **446.** Norman Mailer: "So we think of [the actress] who was every man's love affair with America, [the actress] who was blonde and beautiful and had a

sweet little rinky-dink of a voice and all the clean-
liness of all the clean American backyards. She
was our angel, the sweet angel of sex, and the
sugar of sex came up from her like a resonance of
sound in the clearest grain of a violin. Across five
continents the men who knew the most about love
would covet her, and the classical pimples [!] of
the adolescent working his first gas pump would
also pump for her, since [she] was deliverance, a
very Stradivarius of sex, so gorgeous, forgiving,
humorous, compliant and tender that even the
most mediocre musician would relax his lack of
art in the dissolving magic of her violin. . . . [The
actress] suggested sex might be difficult and dangerous with others, but ice cream with her. If your
taste combined with her taste, how nice, how
sweet. . . . 'Take me,' said her smile. 'I'm easy. I'm
happy. I'm an angel of sex, you bet.' . . . Her stomach, untrammeled by girdles or sheaths, popped
forward in a full woman's belly, inelegant as hell,
an avowal of a womb fairly salivating in seed—
that belly which was never to have a child—and
her breasts popped buds and burgeons of flesh
over many a questing sweating moviegoer's face.
She was a cornucopia. She excited dreams of
honey for the horn. Yet she was more. . . . In her
ambition, so Faustian, and in her ignorance of culture's dimensions, in her liberation and her tyran-
nical desires, her noble democratic longings inti-
mately contradicted by the widening pool of her
narcissism (where every friend and slave must
bathe), we can see the magnified mirror of our-
selves, our exaggerated and now all but defeated
generation, yes, she ran a reconnaissance through
the fifties, and left a message for us in her death,

'Baby go boom.' Now she is the ghost of the sixties."

■ **447.** James Agee: "At the end of [the film] the blind girl who has regained her sight, thanks to the Tramp, sees him for the first time. She has imagined and anticipated him as princely, to say the least; and it has never seriously occurred to him that he is inadequate. She recognizes who he must be by his shy, confident, shining joy as he comes silently toward her. And he recognizes himself, for the first time, through the terrible changes in her face. The camera just exchanges a few quiet close-ups of the emotions which shift and intensify in each face. It is enough to shrivel the heart to see, and it is the greatest piece of acting and the highest moment in movies."

■ **448.** Howard Hughes: "His ears made him look like a taxicab with both doors open."

■ **449.** Ernest Hemingway: "If she had nothing more than her voice she could break your heart with it. But she has that beautiful body and that timeless loveliness of her face. It makes no difference how she breaks your heart if she is there to mend it."

■ **450.** Andrew Sarris: "There are times when [the actor] seems almost too good to be true. His public personality has not altered appreciably since 1959, when he electrified Parisian audiences as a hardboiled Humphrey Bogart worshipper. ... Now, seven years and more than thirty movies later, enough of his easy-going, unpretentious, Rabelaisian personality has seeped across the Atlantic to appeal to those of his campus admirers who are tired of Daddy's heroic declamations on the Great Depression and the Great War. .... Undoubtedly there is something in [the actor], as in Bogart, that deeply disturbs a certain type of authoritarian personality. This something may be largely a myth, but not entirely. In two very different generations a genuinely independent spirit flows out of an actor's apparently casual on-screen gestures. The surface arrogance of both Bogey and [the actor] conceals a tough-guy gallantry underneath. It is no accident that the rediscovery of the forties Bogart has enhanced the reputation of the sixties [the actor], and vice versa. Nevertheless there is much, much more to [the actor] than the Bogey bit. Much more and much less. If at times [the actor] seems like the last of the real movie stars, it is because his extraordinary range encompasses so many different functions and traditions. Who among contemporary actors can simultaneously evoke Douglas Fairbanks and James Dean, Marlon Brando and Marcello Mastroianni, Errol Flynn and John Garfield? Only [the actor], the first actor in film history to combine the intelligence and athleticism of America with the intellectuality and aestheticism of Europe."

☆ ☆ ☆

■ **451.** Name the landmark Western that Louis Lombardo, who edited the film ("3,642 individual cuts—more than any other color film ever made"), is talking about: "The most unconventional thing [the director] did in terms of the soundtrack was to totally redub the sound-effects track after the Kansas City preview. .... All the gunshots—everything: he made [the sound-effects crew] start from scratch. He went in there shouting: 'I want each of these guns to have a different attitude. I want Pike's gun to have a special attitude and I want Ryan's rifle to crack with a different character than [those of] the other bounty hunters on the roof. And I want Strother Martin's gun to be a fuckin' boomer—a buffalo gun.' " Name the director.

■ **452.** She played leading roles in D. W. Griffith's *The Birth of a Nation* in 1915 and *Intolerance* in 1916 and ended her career in John Ford's *Donovan's Reef* in 1963. Vachel Lindsay wrote the following lines about her. Name the actress.

> *She is a Madonna in an art*
> *As wild and young as her sweet eyes,*
> *A cool dew flowers from this hot lamp*
> *That is today's divine surprise.*

■ **453.** Robert Walker costarred in Leo McCarey's *My Son John* but he died not long before the picture was completed. As a result, several shots of Walker in the last reel of McCarey's film were taken from another film, a famous one in which Walker played a psychopath who tries to convince a stranger to "swap" murders with him. Name the picture.

■ **454.** Match the directors in Column A and the composers with whom they often worked in Column B:

COLUMN A	COLUMN B
1 David Lean	**a** Ennio Morricone
2 Sergio Leone	**b** Renzo Rossellini
3 Alfred Hitchcock	**c** Nino Rota

4 Roberto Rossellini   **d** Maurice Jarre
5 Federico Fellini   **e** Bernard Herrmann

■ **455.** In 1960, Raymond Borde and André Bouissy wrote: "The general falling off of neorealism is bound up in great part with the political evolution of Italy. The clerical offensive, the increasingly stringent censorship, the growing hold of the Christian Democrats have played a major role." This statement overlooks the primary reason why neorealism failed to flourish. What is it?

P O S T E R   A D   L I N E S

Name the films being advertised:

■ **456.** "What a glorious feeling!"

■ **457.** "He was 25 years old. He combed his hair like James Dean. He was very fastidious. People who littered bothered him. She was 15. She took music lessons and could twirl a baton. She wasn't very popular at school. For awhile they lived together in a tree house. In 1959, she watched while he killed a lot of people."

■ **458.** "Space Station One: your first step in an Odyssey that will take you to the moon, the planets, and the distant stars."

■ **459.** "The master of suspense weaves his greatest tale! ... about a secret that nobody knew ... a man who never existed ... and a love affair that began in an upper berth—and ended in screaming death."

■ **460.** "Life is a ..."

■ **461.** "The most shocking revenge a girl ever let one brother take on another!"

■ **462.** "He's the highest paid lover in Beverly Hills."

■ **463.** "She's a boy! It's Mr. Hepburn to you!"

■ **464.** " 'To tell you the truth, I ain't a real cowboy. But I'm one helluva stud!' "

■ **465.** "A scandalous record of low Marx at college—or life among the thirsty co-eds!"

QUIZ SIX

☆ ☆

MEMORABLE LINES

Name the films in which the following lines appear as well as the actors who spoke them:

■ **466.** "If anything in this life is certain, if history has taught us anything, it says that you can kill anyone."

■ **467.** "I don't know why he saved my life. Maybe, in those last moments, he loved life more than he ever had before. Not just his life—anybody's life. My life. All he wanted were the same answers the rest of us want: where do I come from? where am I going? how long have I got? All I could do was sit there and watch him die."

■ **468.** "He's very fussy about his drums, you know. They loom large in his legend."

■ **469.** "Your idea of being fulfilled is having more than one man in bed at the same time."

■ **470.** "Arthur said they'd wait for night to do the job, out of respect for second-rate thrillers. 'How do we kill all that time?' asked Odile. Franz had read about an American who'd done the Louvre in nine minutes, forty-five seconds. They'd do better. Arthur, Odile, and Franz beat Jimmy Johnson by two seconds."

☆ ☆ ☆

■ **471.** Directors Raoul Walsh, John Ford, and Erich von Stroheim all played small roles in what classic silent film?

■ **472.** Match the unjustly neglected film in Column A with the commentary on it in Column B:

COLUMN A	COLUMN B
1 John Frankenheimer's *Seconds*	**a** Boy psycho meets teen queen for love, friendship, poignant pretending. As usual, there's trouble with Mom. Funny, complex, violent, moving. A story about America.
2 Edgar G. Ulmer's *Detour*	**b** Guns and gangsters. Terminal men pulped with wit, style, and savagery.
3 Martin Ritt's *The Molly Maguires*	**c** Their love was enough to give paganism a good name. They met and the earth moved enough to produce some dialogue straight from Hemingway Andrew Sarris: "A film that dared to treat

romantic heterosexual love as a sacred subject worthy of epic consideration."

4 Noel Black's
Pretty Poison

d Looks like it cost $25. Plays like $250. But there's a fortune in fatalism bumming around in this silly and soulful King of the Bs.

5 Mike Hodges's
Get Carter

e You're middle-aged tired, fat, and sick of it all, but are you *sure* you want to metamorphose into Rock Hudson almost overnight?

6 Franklin Schaffner's
The War Lord

f *The Informer* meets *Rules of the Game* in a coal mine, and everyone has his reasons.

■ **473.** Some films are great due to the genius of their directors (the *auteur* theory), whereas occasionally a great film (*It's a Wonderful Life*, e.g.) is the result of luck more than anything else, a result of the gelling of the combined efforts of many talents.

This superb film was helmed by an undistinguished director but based on a fine novel (which in most cases means the picture will be mediocre), adapted by Jean-Claude Carriere (who collaborated frequently with Luis Buñuel), shot by Sven Nykvist (Oscar-winning Bergman cinematographer), and beautifully played by Daniel Day-Lewis, Juliette Binoche, and Lena Olin. Name the Czech novelist and the film, which has the same title as the book.

■ **474.** Match the Alfred Hitchcock film in Column A with the famous writer or writers who contributed something—in some cases (e.g., Raymond Chandler), very little—to its screenplay in Column B:

COLUMN A	COLUMN B
1 *Shadow of a Doubt*	**a** James Hilton and Robert Benchley
2 *Frenzy*	**b** Arthur Laurents
3 *Torn Curtain*	**c** Dorothy Parker
4 *Saboteur*	**d** Anthony Shaffer
5 *Notorious*	**e** Maxwell Anderson
6 *North by Northwest*	**f** Raymond Chandler
7 *Rope*	**g** Brian Moore
8 *Strangers on a Train*	**h** Thornton Wilder
9 *The Wrong Man*	**i** Ernest Lehman
10 *Foreign Correspondent*	**j** Ben Hecht

■ **475.** Name the American actor who said: "When I was nineteen years old, I was the number-one star of the world for two years [!?]. When I was forty, nobody wanted me."

A C T O R S O N F I L M

Identify the actors (and in one case the director) being discussed:

■ **476.** François Truffaut: "[The actor's] acting flies in the face of fifty years of filmmaking: each gesture, attitude, each mimicry is a slap at the psychological tradition. [The actor] does not 'show off' the text by understatement like Edwige Feuillère; he does not evoke its poetry, like Gérard Philipe. .. He acts *something beyond* what he is saying. ... He *shifts* his expression from what is being expressed in the way that a consummately modest genius might express profound thoughts self-deprecatingly, as if to excuse himself for his genius, so as not to make a nuisance of himself. . [His] acting is more animal than human, and that makes him unpredictable.   He may, in a single scene, appear to be the son of Frankenstein, a little squirrel, a cowering urchin, or a broken old man. . [The actor's] power of seduction was so intense that he could have killed his parents every night on the screen with the blessing of the snobs and the general public alike   . He killed psychology the day he appeared on the set."

■ **477.** Cecil Beaton: "She has a face that belongs to the sea and the wind, with large rocking-horse nostrils and teeth that you just know bite an apple every day."

■ **478.** Cary Grant: "Cyclically speaking, [the actor] had the same effect on pictures that Marlon Brando had some years later. We did one picture together in 1940. .... [The actor] had the ability to talk naturally. He knew that in conversations people *do* often interrupt one another and that it's not always so *easy* to get a thought out. It took a little while for the sound men to get used to him, but he had an *enormous* impact. And then, some years later, Marlon came out and did the same thing all over again—but what people forget is that [this actor] did it first."

■ **479.** Robin Wood: "One can see what [the director] required by examining any of [the actress's] performances. If one mentally juxtaposes them one realizes that the characterizations are quite distinct from film to film. .... Yet it is equally clear that these characters all relate closely to each other, and to the actress herself, who is being asked to *be* as much as to act. ... In effect, [the director] is encouraging her to draw on her own responses, her own perceptions. None of the roles could be called autobiographical, yet each of them relates significantly to aspects of the actress's personal experience: like Karin, [the actress] was (if voluntarily) a 'displaced person,' like Catherine she had experienced the breakdown of a marriage, like Irene she can be presumed to have felt some guilt at her abeyance of responsibility to her children. To describe the films as 'documentaries on [the actress]' has considerable validity and force. The degree of characterization, of conscious 'acting,' perhaps accounts, paradoxically, for the freedom with which the actress reveals herself, since it avoids the strain and self-consciousness of *cinéme-vérité*. The relationship here between 'acting' and 'being' might be felt to correspond in some way to the relationship between melodrama and documentary in [the director's] films: far from being incompatible, each enhances the other."

■ **480.** François Truffaut: "Having shaved that morning but always in need of a shave, his brows angling toward his temples, eyelids half closed, one hand thrust forward, ready to justify or confound, from film to film [the actor] surveys the length and breadth of life's tribunal, his gait punctuated by Max Steiner's chords. He comes to a stop, spreads his legs a bit, unbuttons his jacket, sticks his thumbs inside his belt, and begins to talk. His clenched jaw indubitably reminds us of the grin of a cheerful corpse, the last expression of a man who is about to die laughing."

☆ ☆ ☆

■ **481.** Francis Coppola directed a number of soft-core porn movies in the sixties before making his first feature film, *Dementia 13*. True or false?

■ **482.** Match each unjustly neglected film in Column A with the commentary on it in Column B:

COLUMN A

1 Joseph H. Lewis's *The Big Combo*

2 Martin Ritt's *Edge of the City*

3 Jacques Rivette's *Paris Belongs to Us*

4 Jack Webb's *Pete Kelly's Blues*

5 Robert Wise's *The Set-Up*

6 Michael Ritchie's *Prime Cut*

7 Tony Richardson's *The Entertainer*

COLUMN B

a Clenched-fists-in-leather *noir* based on a gritty poem by Joseph Moncure March.

b Hot lead, cold sausages, and orphanage flesh in a seriocomic try for the bang-poetry of *Shoot the Piano Player*.

c Now that everybody's crazy for guns, maybe they'll discover this *Laura*-like Lorelei-cop crook mood piece.

d The big Guy's favorite role, and, yes, sir, it's our baby too. That old gray magic.

e If you loved *On the Waterfront* and *The Defiant Ones*, you'll love this one too.

f The *ultimate* film about paranoia.

g The horn man shows some *Gatsby* soul and plays his own version of misty for us.

■ **483.** He began his scriptwriting career working on Bowery Boys movies, was nominated three times for an Academy Award, cowrote David Lean's *The Bridge on the River Kwai* (for which he received no screen credit because of the blacklist), and said of the *auteur* theory: "The screenwriter knows that there is nothing more ludicrous than a director without a screenplay he can *auteur*, like Don Juan without a penis." He is (a) Carl Foreman (b) Dudley Nichols (c) Ernest Lehman (d) Paddy Chayefsky (e) Jules Furthman?

■ **484.** Before each of the characters in Column A died, he, she, or it delivered his, her or its final words to the world in Column B. Match them:

Column A	Column B
1 Anne Bancroft in John Ford's *7 Women*	**a** "I don't want to be disturbed."
2 Orson Welles in Welles's *Citizen Kane*	**b** "Biff, it's very funny. My teeth don't hurt anymore."
3 Charlie Chaplin in Chaplin's *Monsieur Verdoux*	**c** "Lady, I don't have the time."
4 HAL in Stanley Kubrick's *2001: A Space Odyssey*	**d** "So long, you bastard."
5 Clifton Webb in Otto Preminger's *Laura*	**e** "Rosebud!"
6 Alan Hale in Raoul Walsh's *The Strawberry Blonde*	**f** "Ah. Just a moment, I've never tasted rum."
7 Bette Davis in Edmund Goulding's *Dark Victory*	**g** "Good-bye, my love."

8 Lee Marvin in Don Siegel's *The Killers*.

h [Sings] "Daisy, Daisy, give me your answer do/I'm half crazy all for the love of you/It won't be a stylish marriage/I can't afford a carriage/But you'll look sweet/Upon the seat/Of a bicycle built for two."

■ **485.** Name the only silent film to win an Oscar for Best Picture.

P O S T E R   A D   L I N E S

Name the films being advertised:

■ **486.** "What brought a nice kid like Sue Ann to a shocking moment like this?"

■ **487.** "Somebody said *get a life* .. so they did."

■ **488.** "Was he a rebel? Was he a Giant?"

■ **489.** "In a cold world you need your friends to keep you warm."

■ **490.** "A peek into the other woman's male."

QUIZ SIX

MEMORABLE LINES

Name the films in which the following lines appear as well as the actors who spoke them:

■ **491.** "I'm the man who knew Hitler's most secret wishes, his dreams, what he wanted beyond the real world. Every day two or three films: *Broadway Melody* with Fred Astaire, *Snow White* . . Fritz Lang's *Nibelungen*. . . . Whoever controls films controls the future, the world, and he knew it. . . . I know that he was the greatest filmmaker of all time. Again and again, six to eight times in a row he would watch films in order to burn in his memory every frame and every angle. And then I saw him bring the whole thing to a halt at the beginning of the war, no longer looking at feature films but only at newsreels alone with himself, a war made on film exclusively for him."

■ **492.** "Just slip a suppository into position. No such luck for me as a sudden coronary. It has to be slow, squalid, and messy things. Live by the guts, die by the guts. [groans] Now, let science soothe the trouble rectum."

■ **493.** "I like gods. I like them very much. I know exactly how they feel. Exactly."

■ **494.** "Didn't you know? All mild men are vicious. They hate themselves for being mild and they hate the windy extroverts whose violence seems to have a strange attraction for nice girls who should know better."

■ **495.** "Smiley, your words have hair on them."

☆ ☆ ☆

■ **496.** The director, who was also an actor, had just made his first movie. D. W. Griffith came up to him and said, "I am deeply moved, for I have before me the greatest artist in the world." The director-actor glowed. Then Griffith delivered a mortifying clarification: "You're a marvelous actor." Not a word about the picture. Name the movie and its director.

■ **497.** When his contract with Paramount expired in 1936, this actor refused to sign with any studio. Instead, he chose the movies he wanted to do, the directors he wished to work with. Unlike Humphrey Bogart, Jimmy Cagney, or Gary Cooper, he was free to shape and take responsibility for his career. His choices were almost invariably correct, and he became one of the most famous and respected actors in the world. Name him.

■ **498.** Match the directors and films in Column A with the original choices for directors in Column B:

COLUMN A	COLUMN B
1 Sydney Pollack, *Tootsie*	**a** Sergei Eisenstein
2 Joseph Losey, *Eva*	**b** Anthony Mann
3 Anthony Mann, *Winchester '73*	**c** Rouben Mamoulian
4 Francis Coppola, *The Godfather*	**d** Peter Yates
5 Josef von Sternberg, *An American Tragedy*	**e** Sam Peckinpah
6 Burt Reynolds, *Sharky's Machine*	**f** Dick Richards
7 Arthur Penn, *Bonnie and Clyde*	**g** John Boorman
8 Otto Preminger, *Laura*	**h** Fritz Lang
9 Brian De Palma, *Scarface*	**i** Jean-Luc Godard
10 Norman Jewison, *The Cincinnati Kid*	**j** William Wyler
11 Stanley Kubrick, *Spartacus*	**k** François Truffaut
12 John Ford, *How Green Was My Valley*	**l** Sidney Lumet

■ **499.** Probably the most well-known montage expert in movie history, he played Napoleon in Rex Ingram's *Scaramouche*, he and Robert Flaherty directed *The Life and Death of 9413—A Hollywood Extra*, and he designed the montage sequence that opens Ben Hecht's and Charles MacArthur's *Crime Without Passion* as well as designing montages for Frank Capra's *Mr. Smith Goes to Washington*, Jack Conway's *Viva, Villa!*, and Sidney Franklin's *The Good Earth*. He is (a) Lev Kuleshov (b) Robert Wise (c) Don Siegel (d) Karel Reisz (e) Slavko Vorkapich?

■ **500.** Georgie Jessel produced one of the classic *noirs* of the forties, *Nightmare Alley*, which was based on the eponymous novel by William Lindsay Gresham. Gresham's wife was portrayed both by Claire Bloom in a 1985 film and by Debra Winger in a 1993 film. Name them.

A C T O R S   O N   F I L M

Identify the actors being discussed:

■ **501.** Kenneth Tynan: "I have always felt that [the actor] is the finest actor on earth from the neck up."

■ **502.** Herbert Kretzmer: "Boiled down to essentials, she is a plain mortal girl with large feet."

■ **503.** Patricia Bosworth: "His sex appeal is subtle and indirect—his sexuality has a poignancy and a vulnerability, a 'please don't hurt me' quality. He seems to be projecting his own value judgement on the act of love. Behind his beauty is a striving, a determination that keeps him from succumbing completely to narcissism. This inner tension makes [the actor] fascinating to watch. Sex isn't everything, he seems to say with his eyes, it's just a beginning."

■ **504.** William Routt: "[The actor] is Buster Keaton—with power."

■ **505.** Adolph Zukor: "His acting is largely confined to protruding his large, almost occult eyes until the vast areas of white are visible, drawing back the lips of his wide, sensuous mouth to bare his gleaming teeth, and flaring his nostrils."

☆ ☆ ☆

■ **506.** In 1960, Alfred Hitchcock was severely criticized for making a supposedly tasteless and vulgar crime-*cum*-horror film called *Psycho*. That same year, critics practically destroyed the career of a famous British director for making a similarly shocking film. Needless to say, the critics were wrong both times. Name the director and the film.

■ **507.** For five days, Miriam Hopkins believed she was married to a famous German director then working in Hollywood, only to be told by him that the "preacher" was actually a friend of his and the marriage a joke. Name the director.

■ **508.** Match the directors in Column A and the cinematographers with whom they often worked in Column B:

COLUMN A	COLUMN B
1 Ingmar Bergman	**a** Christian Matras
2 Jean-Luc Godard	**b** Sacha Vierny
3 Michelangelo Antonioni	**c** Giuseppe Rotunno
4 Alain Resnais	**d** Raoul Coutard
5 Luchino Visconti	**e** Gianni Di Venanzo
6 Luis Buñuel	**f** Sven Nykvist
7 Claude Chabrol	**g** Marcel Fradetal
8 Sergei Eisenstein	**h** Gabriel Figueroa
9 Max Ophuls	**i** Jean Rabier
10 Georges Franju	**j** Edward Tissé

■ **509.** The first foreign film to win an Oscar was (a) Roberto Rossellini's *Paisan* (b) Ingmar Bergman's *Sawdust and Tinsel/The Naked Night* (c) Marcel Carné's *Les Enfants du paradis* (d) Akira Kurosawa's *Seven Samurai* (e) Vittoria De Sica's *Shoeshine*?

■ **510.** Name the 1980's French film that, in answer to all the George Lucas and Steven Spielberg blockbusters, ends with a postscript that reads: IN MEMORIAM SMALL MOVIES.

P O S T E R   A D   L I N E S

Name the films being advertised:

511. "Vice. And versa ·

512. "Name your poison."

513. "This is the great picture on which the famous co median has worked a whole year."

514. "It's the big one with the big two! They were friends. They were enemies. A passerby could not tell which was who. This was the seething sultry Old Southwest. Where loyalties and labels shifted with the sands, the winking of an eye, the wavering of a gun!"

515. "They're going steady . . . straight to your heart!"

516. "A story about sex, love, tv and   "

517. "The story of a reckless woman!"

518. "When he runs out of dumb luck he always has genius to fall back on."

519. "The story of the strangest vengeance ever planned! She felt his touch—once, and never forgot it! He felt his touch and was turned into a living dead man."

520. "There are no rules."

QUIZ SEVEN

Name the films in which the following lines appear as well as the actors who spoke them:

■ **521.** "No one reads anymore. I have been deprived of my literary right and I crave an audience. The form of the tragic autobiography is dead, or will be soon, along with most of its authors. Goodbye, written word. So I have chosen this form—radio— to author my life. Not because my life is particularly worthy but because it is, hopefully, comically unworthy. Besides, tragedy isn't top forty. Which is just as well."

■ **522.** "Do you want a leg or a breast?"

■ **523.** FIRST ACTOR: "The country's got to make a choice. The time is over for drifters and outlaws and them that's got no backbone."

    SECOND ACTOR: "I'm going to tell you this once, and I don't want to have to say it again. This country's getting old, and I aim to get old with it. Now the Kid

don't want it that way. He might be
a better man for it—I ain't judging.
But I don't want you explaining
nothing to me, and I don't want
you saying nothing about the Kid or
anybody else in my goddamn
country."

■ **524.** "She's my daughter! She's my sister! She's my
daughter! My sister! My daughter! She's my sister
and my daughter!"

■ **525.** "Well, wise up, folks. We're all alone out there,
and tomorrow we're going out there again."

F I L M   C O M M E N T S

Some interesting comments by some interesting people on
some interesting films. Name them:

■ **526.** John Milius: "When I saw Gary Cooper wading
ashore through the waves in the first minutes of
[the film], he became an immediate role model. He
is put ashore . . . for reasons we're never told, except that he has an intense dislike for authority.
On the beach he is met by a crowd of exotic, innocent islanders, who are being ruthlessly sup-
pressed under the regime of a misguided Christian
missionary. . . . Mr. Morgan (Cooper) only wants to
be left alone, but he is a glaring example of individual will to the others and must be made to bow
and kiss the ring. Not Gary Cooper, no way.
You're dealing with Yankee independence. . . Besides, he has a shotgun. His hut is eventually torn
down and he asks the community, 'Who will help
put it back up?' In a scene that's etched in my

memory forever, a simple dark-eyed girl steps forward where all the others cower. This is romance. this is love. Nothing else will really do. . . . With the aid of the shotgun, Mr. Morgan becomes the unwitting instrument of revolt. The people are freed, the wardens banished. . . . An idealized society, no government, lots of food, sex, surf, and the intoxicating sound of the drums and the dances. Of course, it is here that Conrad always warns us that white men go bad—at the point of moral choice. They either lose control like Mr. Kurtz, or drift on because they have no anchor. . . . Mr. Morgan is the latter. He never marries the girl. She dies bearing him a daughter; he realizes he's lost the only thing he ever had, and leaves embittered. . . . Cooper wanders the winds, becoming a hardened, friendless man. World War II starts and something brings him back. He returns to the island to find himself a legend of the past, a part of . . . history and folklore. He also finds his daughter and, eventually, himself. In this final, sentimental confrontation, he discovers what all adventurers and drifters really seek, that which most people had all along—a home. It's a simple powerful emotion, one that the cynicism in all of us constantly tries to reject. But it gnaws at the back of my heart and has colored all of my work. I've written parts and shades of this story into everything I've ever really cared about, from *Jeremiah Johnson* to *Conan*. I guess I do it unconsciously. Maybe it's just because I, too, really want to be like Gary Cooper at the end of the movie: standing on the dock, listening to the music with my arm around my daughter, and letting the boat sail away without me."

■ **527.** Akira Kurosawa: "I can never forget the excitement in my mind after seeing [the film]. I have had several more opportunities to see the film since then and each time I feel more overwhelmed. It is the kind of cinema that flows with the serenity and nobility of a big river. People are born, live out their lives, and then accept their deaths. Without the least effort and without any sudden jerks, [the director] paints his picture, but its effect on the audience is to stir up deep passions. How does he achieve this? There is nothing irrelevant or haphazard in his cinematographic technique. In that lies the secret of its excellence."

■ **528.** William S. Pechtler: "As George Bailey, the film's hero, jumps into the river to commit suicide as the culmination of his progress of disastrous failures, he is saved ... by an angel! This is, of course, the perfect, and, in fact, only alternative for [the director]; and the *deus ex machina* serves its classic purpose ... namely to satisfy an understanding of the work on every level. It creates, for those who wish it, the happy ending par excellence. ... Yet, for those who can accept the realities of George Bailey's situation—the continual frustration of his ambitions, his envy of those who have done what he has only wanted to do, the collapse of his business, a sense of utter isolation, final despair—and do not believe in angels, ... the film ends, in effect, with the hero's suicide. [The film] is the kind of work that defies criticism; almost, one might say, defies art. It is one of the funniest and one of the bleakest, as well as being one of the most technically adroit, films ever made; it is a masterpiece, yet rather of that kind peculiar to the film: unconscious masterpieces. Consciously, except in the matter of his certainly conscious concern with the mastery of his medium's technique, I don't imagine [the director] conceives of himself as much different than Clarence Budington Kelland. ... [The film] is a truly subversive work, the *Huckleberry Finn* which gives the lie to the *Tom Sawyer*s; yet I am certain [the director] would not think of it in this way, nor boast of pacts made with the devil."

■ **529.** Robin Wood: "[The film] is the most fully realized and satisfying of the 'period' epics with which Hollywood in the early sixties faced the challenge of television. ... Its central theme is the cost of heroism: the way in which demands made on the heroic figure deprive him of his flexible, living humanity, until he ends as (literally) a rigid corpse strapped to a horse, leading his men to victory."

■ **530.** Andrew Sarris: "I happen to admire ... [the film] even though many people whose opinions I respect don't like the movie and many people whose opinions I suspect do. Furthermore, the main anti-argument (pretentiousness) strikes a more responsive chord in my critical temperament than does the pro-argument (realism). [The film] is photographed through a test-pattern haze of pea soup, and much of the dialogue is thrown away so hard it bounces. It is true that a large part of [the director's] originality is more peculiar than effective. ... Nonetheless, [the film] succeeds, almost in spite of itself, with a rousing finale which is less symbolic summation than poetic evocation of the fierce aloneness in American life. I can't remember when I have been so moved by something which has left me so uneasy to the marrow of my aesthetic. Unlike so many of his contemporaries, [the director] tends to lose battles and win wars. Indeed, of how many other films can you say that the whole is better than its parts? [The actor's] reluctant hero and [the actress's] matter-of-fact $5 whore are nudged from bumptious farce through black comedy all the way to solitary tragedy imbedded in the communal indifference with which [the director] identifies America. ... I disagree, however, with those ... who see [the director's] achievement as the final nail in the coffin of the Western genre. Quite the contrary. The best moments in [the film] owe their majestic splendor to the moral integrity and psychological implacability of the Western genre. Ultimately, [the film] shapes up as a half-baked masterpiece with a kind of gutsy grandeur. It's personal as all-get-out, and I thought that's what everyone had been screaming for all these years."

☆ ☆ ☆

■ **531.** This cycle of seven small-budget Westerns (1956–60)—all directed by Budd Boetticher, all starring Randolph Scott—has gained considerable critical acclaim over the years. These movies (which featured personable, good-bad-but-not-evil villains) are usually referred to as a specific series, the name of which was formed by using the first part of its star's name and the last part of its producer's. Name the series.

■ **532.** Name the American actor-director who said: "I don't want to achieve immortality through my work. I want to achieve immortality by not dying."

■ **533.** Name the comedy team that Charles Barr was writing about: "They are a pair of overgrown babies who, in Freudian terms, have not grasped the reality principle: they have not learned to separate their own ego from the outside world."

■ **534.** From its start in a Milwaukee nickelodeon in 1909 through the sale of its Hollywood facilities to Lucille Ball's and Desi Arnaz's Desilu Productions in 1953, the studio had a strange and somewhat shaky history: innumerable corporate mergings at the beginning, Howard Hughes at the end. Still, in the thirties and forties, there were the Fred Astaire-Ginger Rogers musicals, Orson Welles's *Citizen Kane* and *The Magnificent Ambersons*, Alfred Hitchcock's *Suspicion*, and Jacques Tourneur's *Out of the Past*. Name the studio.

■ **535.** Name the only actor or actress who ever won an Oscar for playing a member of the opposite sex.

O N D I R E C T O R S

Name the directors (and, in one case, the two films) being discussed:

■ **536.** Robert Mitchum: "He used to hang around out at Astoria studios. Now he goes to UFA and tells 'em he's a great American director and he gets a job and makes a couple of films in German. Now he comes back to this country and he's a great German director. He affects a German accent. He has green suede trousers and berets and a long cigarette holder and an apple box to stand on 'cause he's like four foot nothin'."

■ **537.** Robin Wood: "Renoir said of [the director] that he was one of the best American directors because he really understood people. ... Both [the director's] excellence and his limitations can be suggested by juxtaposing his work with Renoir's. . . . One aspect of the understanding of people in their films is the understanding of actors: the work of both is actor-centered. One might contrast the cinema of Renoir, [the director], and Hawks with that of Hitchcock, Sternberg, and Antonioni. Hitchcock denies that he said actors are cattle: he said they should be *treated* like cattle. To Sternberg, actors are 'puppets'; and to Antonioni, in the words of Arthur Penn, they are 'beautiful statuary.' To Renoir, [the director], and Hawks they are responsive human beings, with particular gifts, particular limitations, particular reactions, out of which the film develops: that is the foundation of their 'humanism.' Some of the most delightful scenes in the American cinema grew directly out of [the director's] creative collaboration with his actors, even out of his knowledge of their limitations. Witness the famous scene in [the first film] where Leila Hyams teaches Roland Young to play the drums; or the 'Home on the Range' scene in [the second film], improvised on the first day of shooting when [the director] discovered that Ralph Bellamy couldn't sing and Irene Dunne was an inexpert pianist. . . . If Renoir must ultimately be judged the superior artist (though I feel for his films no greater affection than for [the director's] best work), the judgment must be founded on the fact that he achieves what [the director] does not, a visual style that in itself expresses a metaphysic, a personal view of life."

■ **538.** Manny Farber: "One director in particular has made his living by subjecting the film audience to a series of cheap, glossy, mechanically perfect shocks, and for this he has been hailed as the High Boojum of Suspense. The name of this artist is, of course, [the director]—who has gone farther on fewer brains than any director since Griffith, while cleverly masking his deficiency and his underlying petty and pointless sadism with a honey-smooth patina of 'sophistication,' irony and general glitter."

■ **539.** Jean-Pierre Coursodon: "While [the director] was the last of the contract directors .. he was by no means a studio hack, and unless one takes an unreasonably radical view of the American film business at the time, never behaved as the 'slave' François Truffaut scornfully accused him of being. He may have worked on assignment throughout his career, yet his filmography indicates a high level of selectivity. [The director] was, indeed, one of the most highly specialized among Hollywood's major-league directors. One simply can't imagine a [the director]-directed Western, thriller, adventure film, or war epic (even though he did dabble in the latter genre . . .). [The director's] specialization, however, was not a genre, since he shuttled with the greatest of ease between comedy and drama, but rather a mood. . . . [The director] brought new life to the Hollywood musical at MGM quite some time before Gene Kelly and Stanley Donen (or Charles Walters), and despite all the shared resources, they tapped thoroughly different lodes. The Kelly-Donen pictures, like all the Kelly-starring musicals before them, are down-to-earth, brash, plebeian, and indomitably mirthful. [The director's] on the other hand, are ethereal (Kelly's .. term), dreamlike, nostalgic, and melancholy."

■ **540.** Andrew Sarris: "[The director's] cinema is the cinema of the nightmare, the fable, and the philosophical dissertation. His plots generally go inexplicably sour or sentimental at the very end. ... What we remember in Renoir are the faces of Gabin, Simon, and Ledoux. What we remember in [the director] are the geometrical patterns of tracks, trains, and fateful camera angles. If Renoir is humanism, [the director] is determinism. If Renoir is concerned with the plight of his characters, [the director] is obsessed with the structure of the trap."

P O S T E R   A D   L I N E S

Name the films being advertised:

■ **541.** "Blood red kisses! White-hot thrills! Mickey Spillane's latest H-Bomb!"

■ **542.** "Watch out! The almighty J.J. ... the columnist with sixty million believers ... his wrath is feared by the great and near great who worship the ..."

■ **543.** "For the first time, Alfred Hitchcock goes to real life for his thrills!"

■ **544.** "In the media circus of life, they were the main attraction."

■ **545.** "YOU accept an invitation to a blonde's apartment! YOU get socked in the jaw by a murder suspect! YOU slug the crooked cop who tries to frame you! YOU look into the gun of a fear-maddened killer! Starring *YOU* and Robert Montgomery."

QUIZ SEVEN
☆ ☆

M E M O R A B L E   L I N E S

Name the films in which the following lines appear as well as the actors who spoke them:

■ **546.** "Hey, shithead, when was the last time you picked your feet, huh? I got a man in Poughkeepsie wants to talk to you. ... You been in Poughkeepsie, haven't you? I want to hear it, come on! You been there, right? ... You sat on the edge of the bed, didn't you? You took off your shoes, put your finger between your toes and picked your feet, didn't you? Well, say it! ... Now I'm gonna bust your ass for those three bags and I'm gonna nail you for picking your feet in Poughkeepsie."

■ **547.** "Get out of my way, Johnny, I'm gonna spit!"

■ **548.** "Girls, what's that? Look! It's Jesus!"

■ **549.** "Men that I know—and I've known dozens of them—they're so nice, so polite, so considerate. Most women like that type. I guess they're afraid of the other type. I thought I was too, but you're so strong. You don't give, you take! Oh, Tommy! I could love you to death!"

■ **550.** "Time, time, what is time? Swiss manufacture it, French hoard it, Italians squander it, Americans say it is money, Hindus say it does not exist. You know what I say? I say time is a crook."

F I L M   C O M M E N T S
Some interesting comments by some interesting people on some interesting films. Name them:

■ **551.** Stanley Kubrick: "Confront a man in his office with a nuclear alarm and you have a documentary. If the news reaches him in his livingroom, you have a drama. If it catches him in the lavatory, the result is comedy."

■ **552.** Pauline Kael: "An elegy for a wasted life, adapted by [the director] from a thirties novel, [the film] dealt with the forty-eight hours before the suicide of a dissolute playboy ... who, at thirty, has outlived his boyish charm and his social credit. It is a study of despair with no possibility of relief; the man has used up his slim resources and knows it. He does not want to live as what he has become; his taste is too good. It was directed in a clean, deliberate style, with a lone piano playing Satie in the background. Genet wrote of the director, 'He has effected something phenomenal this time, having turned literature into film, photographed the meaning of an insubstantial, touching, and rather famous book, and given its tragic intention a clarity it never achieved in print.' And Brendan Gill said, 'Between them, [the director] and [the actor] have composed a work as small and vast, as affecting, and I think, as permanent as Fitzgerald's *Babylon Revisited*.' It was a masterly film, and it seemed almost inconceivable that a director still so young could produce a work about such anguish with such control. [The film] should have made [the director's] reputation here—in the way that *L'avventura* made Antonioni's."

■ **553.** Andrew Sarris: "Connoisseurs of thirties horror films know that the real gem ... was [the film] with [the director's] bizarre camera angles battling Ernest Thesiger's fruity performance for attention."

■ **554.** Robin Wood: "[The director] is often accused of sentimentality: I think the charge may be partly a defense against the embarrassingly direct and simple emotional appeal his films frequently make. How many directors would have allowed Beulah Bondi to recite an entire sentimental poem to her husband in the hotel restaurant in [the film]? (But how many would have dared make that extraordinarily honest and desolating film at all?) The sentimentality, here, is in the poem, not the scene, the context of which places and comments on the sort of comfort the poem offers. The film, in fact, is as remarkable for its toughness as it is for the emotional generosity that some call 'sentimental.' "

■ **555.** Martin Scorsese: "When I first saw it, as a kid, [the film] became my favorite film. I'd always been addicted to historical epics, but this one was different: it gave the sense that we were really there. *This* is the way people lived; *this* is what they believed, thought, and felt. You get it through the overall look of the picture: the low ceilings, the torchlit interiors, the shape of the pillars, the look of the extras. There's a marvelous moment when the dead are being taken away from battle in their coffins, and someone says, 'Let us hear the gods of Egypt speak.' The camera pans over to one of the statues of the gods, and it talks. That's it—the statue talks! You don't see the mouth moving, you just hear the voice. Then they pan over to the other god—and now *he* talks. Soon there are about four gods talking. You're never told, 'this is how they did it: it was a joke, a trick.' In a sense, you're taken into confidence by the Egyptians; you're let in on a religion. I watch this film over and over again."

☆ ☆ ☆

■ **556.** Match the unjustly neglected film in Column A with the commentary on it in Column B:

COLUMN A

1 Ben Hecht's
Specter of the Rose

2 Joseph Losey's
These Are the Damned

COLUMN B

a He was hundreds of years old and lived under a curse. Her namesake was the mythological woman created by the gods to bring ruin to men. Love at first sight.

b It's your regiment until some upper-class toff replaces you as commanding officer. What to do? Drive him to suicide.

3 Don Levy's
Herostratus

c You've seen it on TV and loved it, but you *can't* remember the title. It's the one about the spaceship found buried in aLondon subway.

4 Ronald Neame's
Tunes of Glory

d The love story of a mad ballet dancer and a ballerina. He wants to kill her. Instead he jumps out the window of a skyscraper, doing entrechats as he falls.

5 Albert Lewin's
Pandora and the Flying Dutchman

e Bleak Norwegian skies. Religious repression. Insanity in the family. He literally tried to brush it all away.

6 Roy Ward Baker's
Five Million Years to Earth

f Teddy-boy rebels, a sci-fi cave under the rocks by the sea, an American tourist and a girl, haunted sculptress, well-meaning but evil politician, and strange, sad, radioactive children.

7 Peter Watkins's
Edvard Munch

g A young poet turned cynical by society decides to kill himself. But he wants to be remembered. So he "sells" his death to an ad agency.

■ **557.** Name the French pioneer director-producer whose motto was "Life as it is lived."

■ **558.** Match the actors or actresses and films in Column A with the original choices for the roles in Column B:

COLUMN A	COLUMN B
1 James Coburn in Sam Peckinpah's *Major Dundee*	**a** Moira Shearer
2 Edmund Purdom in Michael Curtiz's *The Egyptian*	**b** Marlon Brando
3 Melvyn Douglas in Ernst Lubitsch's *Ninotchka*	**c** Al Pacino
4 Albert Finney in John Huston's *Under the Volcano*	**d** William Powell
5 Elizabeth Taylor in Richard Brooks's *Cat on a Hot Tin Roof*	**e** Grace Kelly
6 Humphrey Bogart in Archie Mayo's *The Petrified Forest*	**f** Montgomery Clift
7 Richard Gere in Francis Coppola's *The Cotton Club*	**g** Lee Marvin
8 Shirley MacLaine in Don Siegel's *Two Mules for Sister Sara*	**h** Richard Burton
9 Gary Cooper in Fred Zinneman's *High Noon*	**i** Edward G. Robinson
10 Cyd Charisse in Vincente Minnelli's *Brigadoon*	**j** Elizabeth Taylor

■ **559.** In the sixties, Andrew Sarris's choice for "the most romantic title in the history of the cinema" was (a) D. W. Griffith's *Broken Blossoms* (b) D. W. Griffith's *Orphans of the Storm* (c) Frank Borzage's *History Is Made at Night* (d) Charlie Chaplin's *City Lights* (e) Orson Welles's *Chimes at Midnight*?

■ **560.** Match the unjustly neglected film in Column A with the commentary on it in Column B:

COLUMN A

1 Gillo Pontecorvo's *Burn!*

2 John Flynn's *The Outfit*

3 Peter Bogdanovich's *Saint Jack*

4 Michael Reeves's *Conqueror Worm/The Witchfinder General*

5 Roger Corman's *Tomb of Ligeia*

6 Robert Aldrich's *Ulzana's Raid*

COLUMN B

a That *Walking Tall* guy and Col. Kilgore spray vengeful lead at or around these *noir* icons: R. Ryan, T. Cary, S. North, J. Greer, M. Windsor, E. Cook, Jr. —and more!

b A truly first-rate Vincent Price horror movie? Best of this series. Written by Robert Towne.

c A Vietnam fable or a film *really* about fighting the savages, whoever they are? Both.

d A British agent teaches tropical blacks how to stage a revolution. Ten years later, for pay, he terminates the same revolution.

e The whorehouse *Great Gatsby* of Southeast Asia.

f A truly first-rate Vincent Price horror movie? Not really a horror movie, though its violence is extreme and its mood as bleak as you'd expect from a twenty-five-year-old director who committed suicide.

O N D I R E C T O R S
•••

Identify the directors (and, in one case, the three films) being discussed:

■ **561.** Jean-Luc Godard: "With him, French neorealism was born. Yes, this moon-man is a poet. ... He sees problems where there are none, and finds them. He is capable of filming a beach scene simply to show that children building a sandcastle drown the sound of the waves with their cries. He will also shoot a scene just because at that moment a window is opening in a house away in the background, and a window opening—well, that's funny. This is what interests [the director]. Everything and nothing ... everything which is at once real, bizarre, and charming. [The director] has a feeling for comedy because he has a feeling for strangeness."

■ **562.** Manny Farber: "Hollywood's fair-haired boy, to the critics, is [the director]; in terms of falling into the Hollywood mold, he is a smooth blend of iconoclast and sheep. If you look at his films, what appears to be a familiar story, face, grouping of actors, or tempo has in each case an obscure, outrageous, double-crossing unfamiliarity that is the product of an Eisenstein-lubricated brain. He has a personal reputation as a bad-boy, a homely one (called 'Double-Ugly' by friends, 'monster' by enemies), who has been in every known trade, rugged or sedentary. ... His films, which should be rich with this extraordinary experience, are rich with cut-and-dried homilies; expecting a mobile and desperate style, you find stasis manipulated with the surehandedness of a Raffles."

■ **563.** Jim Kitses: "[The director's] response to the Western was not a response to history, as with Ford and Peckinpah, but to its archetypal form, the mythic patterns deeply imbedded in the plots and characters of the genre that can shape the action. ... The agrarian ideal, so central to Ford, has little relevance for [the director's] work. ... [The director's] West is a wilderness, 'way up in that far country,' where the passions he deals with can find expression, his conflicts their resolutions. ... From beginning to end, the characters of [the director] are extreme men stretching beyond their reach. Rarely is it a matter of choice: as if possessed, these men push ahead completely at the mercy of forces within themselves. ... [The director's] hero is a revenge hero ... [and] the revenge taken by the character is taken *upon* himself, a punishment the inner meaning of which is a denial of reason and humanity. ... Trapped in an impossible dilemma, a neurotic attempt to escape themselves and rise above a past of pain and violence, [the director's] heroes are *brought low*, driven ... to face themselves, reliving the experiences they flee. ... The universe they inhabit is one of rushing rivers and the lonely, brutal rocks of the snowline. ... At times [the director's] cinema reaches an electrifying pitch in the relentless way it focuses on ... a horrific landscape. ... The terrain is so colored by the action that it finally seems an inner landscape, the unnatural world of a disturbed mind."

■ **564.** Vsevold Meyerhold: "In [the director] the predominant element is tragedy; in Chaplin it is pathos. Pushkin called laughter, pity, and terror the three strings of our imagination that the magic of the drama sets vibrating. In Chaplin laughter and pity take precedence, while terror remains muted. In [the director] pity and terror predominate over laughter."

■ **565.** Robin Wood: "In several of [the director's] best films there is a character who, one feels, is accorded a special status. He is always a minor character, more spectator than participant, detached, belonging to no one, but well-disposed, looking on perceptively and intelligently and acting decisively at crucial moments, when his participation is necessary: the deaf-and-dumb boy in [the first film], a *film noir* that is related interestingly, with its world of shadows and uncertainties, to horror fantasies; the mandolin-playing singer ... in [the second film]. These are perhaps the characters to whom [the director] is closest. Related to them is Carrefour, ... of [the third film], one of [the director's] most haunting characters, guardian of the crossroads, speechless intermediary between the shadowy other-world and the world of consciousness, at once knowing and unknowing; the enigma at the heart of [the director's] universe."

P O S T E R   A D   L I N E S

Name the films being advertised:

■ **566.** "Do you know what I do to squealers? I let them have it in the belly. So they can roll around for a long time thinking it over."

■ **567.** "The star-spangled, laugh-loaded salute to our P.O.W. heroes."

■ **568.** "If a woman answers ... hang on for dear life!"

■ **569.** "She was born into a world where they called it seduction not rape. What she did would shatter that world forever. As timely today as the day it was written."

■ **570.** "Nobody knew where he came from. But he was the best they'd ever seen."

QUIZ SEVEN

★ ★ ☆

M E M O R A B L E   L I N E S

Name the films in which the following lines appear as well as the actors who spoke them:

■ **571.** ACTRESS: "And love?"
   ACTOR: "Those who believe in love can find a woman."
   ACTRESS: "Is that happiness?"
   ACTOR: "Happiness does not exist. What one talks about most exists the least."

■ **572.** "I am impotent and I like it!"

■ **573.** "That's one of the tragedies in this life—that the men who are most in need of a beating-up are always enormous."

■ **574.** "The last six months were excruciating. He obviously saw it was all over, felt it at least but wouldn't accept it. .. He tried to keep the wife, if not wholly, then in bed. I let him possess me, I bore it. ... That man was filth to me. He stank—stank like a man. What had once had its charms now turned my stomach, brought tears to my eyes. .. The way he bestraddled me, servicing me like a bull

168

would a cow. Not the least respect, no feeling for a woman's pleasure. The pain you can't imagine."

■ **575.** "He was some kind of a man. What does it matter what you say about people."

D I R E C T O R S   O N   F I L M

Identify the directors doing the talking:

■ **576.** "My films are a declaration of war against the present forms of cinema dialogue and of boulevard-type cinema in the tradition of Hollywood and its satellites. . . . A declaration of war against psychological chitchat, against the action film, against a particular philosophy endlessly linking shots and reverse shots, against the metaphysics of the automobile and the gun, against the excitement of opened and closed doors, against the melodrama of crime and sex."

■ **577.** "My primary concern in a film is to prevent the images from flowing, to oppose them to each other, to anchor them and join them. . . . It is precisely that deplorable flow that is called 'cinema' by the critics, who mistake it for style."

■ **578.** "New American films are just like television in the way they tie you to the screen. The loose bonds are getting tighter all the time. I keep having this physical sensation of being tied all the time—as though there were cables running from the screen to each seat. Like a dog on a leash, that's what it's like in the cinema nowadays; and I can understand a dog wanting to get free of its leash. Great cinema let people off their leashes. In John Ford's films, say, you were up there on the screen in that great openness. Television keeps the leads tight, otherwise people would keep changing the channel.

"Americans have given up experiencing life outside the cinema and as a result they're unable to get anything of life into their films. I read a very frank interview with Steven Spielberg. He said he thought it was a great loss to himself that his entire experience, his world, consisted entirely of his childhood cinema experiences. It's an astonishing admission."

■ **579.** "I have rid myself of much unnecessary technical baggage, eliminating all the logical narrative transitions, all those connective links between sequences where one sequence served as a springboard for the one that followed. The reason I did this was because it seemed to me that cinema should be tied to the truth rather than to logic. . . . I think it is important for cinema to turn toward internal forms of filmmaking, towards ways of expression that are absolutely free."

■ **580.** "I'm not really a director. I'm a man who believes in the validity of a person's inner desires. And I think those inner desires, whether they're ugly or beautiful, are pertinent to each of us and are probably the only things worth a damn. I want to put those inner desires on the screen so we can all look and think and feel and marvel at them. I've been concerned from the beginning with the problems confronting real people rather than emphasizing dramatic structure or bending characters to the plot. The studio system just doesn't suit me. It's a system based on departments and department heads and I'm not very good at dealing with department heads.

"I feel we have to move beyond the current obsession with technique and camera angles. It's a waste of time. How you shoot a film is a diversion. I think anybody can shoot a film. Look at the most commercial things in the world—television commercials. They're magnificently photographed. What are we wasting our time doing that for? It has nothing to do with life. We're making that a value. Pretty photography is part of our culture.

"I'm not part of anything. I never joined anything. I'm an individual. Intellectual bullshit doesn't interest me. I'm only interested in working with people who like to work and finding out about something they don't already know. I don't care what the problems'll be as long as I stay crazy. I mean, I'm basically a bum. I know a lot of my enemies would agree with that. But I don't think that's such a bad thing. I think it's more fun. I think I probably have the philosophy of a poor man. You know, like maybe I'd steal the pennies off a dead man's eyes."

☆ ☆ ☆

■ **581.** In a 1958 *Cahiers du cinéma* poll, this film was voted "the most beautiful film in the world." It was (a) Victor Sjöström's *The Wind* (b) Buster Keaton's and Clyde Bruckman's *The General* (c) Max Ophuls's *La Ronde* (d) Jean Renoir's *La Règle du jeu* (e) F. W. Murnau's *Sunrise*?

■ **582.** Until the early 'fifties, movie stars were paid a straight fee and never shared in the profits of their pictures. Then everything changed. A major actor, about to sign up for a Western, agreed to take less than his usual salary in exchange for a percentage of the profits, if any. The star collected a tidy bundle. Needless to say, this kind of deal soon became the norm, and stars began to call the shots. The actor and the movie were (a) John Wayne in John Ford's *Rio Grande* (b) Kirk Douglas in Howard Hawks's *The Big Sky* (c) Jimmy Stewart in Anthony Mann's *Bend of the River* (d) Alan Ladd in George Stevens's *Shane* (e) Robert Mitchum in Otto Preminger's *River of No Return*?

■ **583.** Match the name of the film in Column A with its working title in Column B:

COLUMN A

1 Alfred Hitchcock's *Vertigo*
2 John Huston's *The Maltese Falcon*
3 John Farrow's *His Kind of Woman*
4 Henry Hathaway's *The House on 92nd Street*
5 Nicholas Ray's *In a Lonely Place*
6 Arthur Penn's *Night Moves*
7 Nicholas Ray's *On Dangerous Ground*
8 Alfred Hitchcock's *North by Northwest*
9 Nicholas Ray's *They Live by Night*
10 Fritz Lang's *While the City Sleeps*
11 Elia Kazan's *Panic in the Streets*

COLUMN B

a *The Dark Tower*

b *News Is Made at Night*

c *Now it Can Be Told*

d *Breathless*

e *Smiler With a Gun*

f *Behind This Mask*

g *The Gent From Frisco*

h *Night Cry*

i *From Amongst the Dead*

j *Outbreak*

k *Mad With Much Heart*

12 Otto Preminger's *Where* | *Your Red Wagon*
   the *Sidewalk Ends*

■ **584.** In the midthirties, there were sometimes as many as twelve movies nominated for an Oscar as Best Picture. Later, ten. In what year was the number stabilized at five?

■ **585.** Name the famous director who, when asked about his ability to discover beautiful unknown actresses, replied: "I suppose it's because I was born with two crystal balls."

O N   D I R E C T O R S

Identify the directors being discussed:

■ **586.** Jean-Luc Godard: "There was theatre (Griffith), poetry (Murnau), painting (Rossellini), dance (Eisenstein), music (Renoir). Henceforth there is cinema. And the cinema is [the director]."

■ **587.** François Truffaut: "[The director] is so terribly solemn, so terribly pompous. I don't like the image he projects of himself as *the* psychologist of the feminine soul. When de Gaulle was trying to restore the confidence of the French in Algeria, he said, 'French men and women, I have understood you.' [The director] stands like that and says, 'Women of the world, I have understood you.' "

■ **588.** Michelangelo Antonioni: "[The director's] films are like a river, lovely to see, to bathe in, extraordinarily refreshing and pleasant then the water flows and is gone. Very little of the pleasant feeling remains because I soon feel dirty again and need another bath. ... His images are   power-ful ... but his stories are frivolous."

■ **589.** Joseph L. Mankiewicz: "To me, the so-called film historians, the film critics who look for transcendental meanings in the work of men who couldn't spell the word transcendental, I call them the emperor's tailors. They're busy making this invisible clothing. Poor [the director] suddenly finds himself full of all sorts of political implications when he didn't have them at all. It was just a good screenplay that was handed to him ... and he directed it with exactly the same psychological input as he did the Harry Langdon comedies."

■ **590.** Robin Wood: "[The director's] is a cinema built on tensions and paradoxes. A gentle, sensitive, civilized man, he has made films notorious for their violence. His general orientation is towards author-director's cinema, the European art-film, and he admits to idolizing Ingmar Bergman: yet his films are intensely American in subject-matter and usually rooted in the traditions of genre cinema. ... The richness of his films arises ... above all from the remarkably alive, responsive performances he elicits from his actors. ... Through all this one can trace a coherent psychological pattern: on the one hand a reliance on, and respect for, the instinctual ... on the other, a persistent yearning after intellectual control. ... This psychological pattern is reflected in the films, which consistently express in dramatic terms the struggle between the 'holiness' of the first (in Blake's sense: 'Everything that *lives* is holy') counterbalanced by the necessity for the second. ... The hiatuses in [the director's] work may suggest the increasing difficulties he has in affirming anything or even in offering confident statements. Yet he remains an immensely sympathetic figure, with a relatively small but vital body of work that demands recognition and respect."

P O S T E R   A D   L I N E S

Name the films being advertised:

591. "Nothing ever held you like its suspense! Nothing ever held you like its false love! From beginning to end, nothing ever held you like . . ."

592. "She had blood in her veins . . . he had ink and guts! The picture with the page one punch!"

593. "The only thing greater than their passion for America . . . was their passion for each other."

594. "Pass the warning."

595. "He's a killer when he hates!"

596. "They caught all hell—and hurled it back—at . . ."

■ 597. "Showdown in the high Sierra!"

■ 598. "You look at the Italian shoes and the turtleneck and you have to wonder. You listen to the official beefs about 'personal misconduct,' 'disruptive influence,' you figure he's got to be up for trade."

599. "The epic of the American doughboy."

600. "Her soft mouth was the road to sin-smeared violence."

QUIZ EIGHT

M E M O R A B L E   L I N E S

Name the films in which the following lines appear and in some cases the actors who spoke them:

■ **601.** "Forty-two percent of all liberals are queer. The Wallace people took a poll."

■ **602.** "This film tells the story of a man who was the first to unite our country four hundred years ago: the Archduke of Moscow who wielded greedy, warring, and divided principalities into a single powerful State, a military leader who made the glory of Russian arms resound in the East as in the West, a sovereign who resolved his country's cruel dilemmas by having himself crowned the first Tsar of all the Russias."

■ **603.** "Live fast, die young, and have a good looking corpse."

■ **604.** "In Italy, for thirty years under the Borgias, they had warfare, terror, murder, bloodshed—they produced Michelangelo, Leonardo da Vinci, and the Renaissance In Switzerland, they had brotherly love, five hundred years of democracy and peace, and what did they produce? The cuckoo clock."

■ **605.** "This is the West, sir. When legend becomes fact, print the legend."

■ **606.** ACTRESS: "Wait for what?"

ACTOR: "For the sound of the fire alarm, Miss Flagg—waiting to go rushing off to the fire."

ACTRESS: "What fire is that, Mr. Cook?"

ACTOR: "Love . . ."

ACTRESS: "Are you looking for a big fire, skipper, or just a little one made out of strawberry boxes and lies?"

ACTOR: "It doesn't matter. It's usually out before your hook and ladder gets there."

■ **607.** " 'No, I can't go back, I can't! They are horrible! It was all horrible! They don't know what they're doing. I'm even worse. . . . I'll save him, my innocent child. . . . God! My God, help me! Give me the strength, the courage . . . oh my God, merciful God!' '

■ **608.** "Would you like me to tell you the little story of Right-Hand-Left-Hand—the story of Good and Evil? H-A-T-E! It was with his left hand that old brother Cain struck the blow that laid his brother low! L-O-V-E! You see these fingers, dear hearts? These fingers has veins that run straight to the soul of a man! The right hand, friends! The hand of Love! Now watch and I'll show you the Story of Life. These fingers, dear hearts, is always a-warrin' and a-tuggin' one hand agin' t'other. No,

watch 'em! Old Brother Left Hand. Left Hand
Hate's a-fightin', and it looks like Love's a goner!
But wait a minute!! Wait! a minute! Hot dog!
Love's a-winnin'! Yessirree! It's Love that won!
And old Left Hand Hate is down for the count!"

A C T O R S   O N   F I L M

Identify the actors (and, in one case, the actor and the film)
being discussed:

■ **609.** James Agee: "[The actor's] face ranked almost
with Lincoln's as an early American archetype; it
was haunting, handsome, almost beautiful, yet it
was irreducibly funny; he improved matters by
topping it off with a deadly horizontal hat, as flat
and thin as a phonograph record. One can never
forget [the actor] wearing it, standing erect at the
prow as his little boat is being launched. The boat
goes grandly down the skids and, just as grandly,
straight on to the bottom. [The actor] never
budges. The last you see of him, the water lifts the
hat off the stoic head and it floats away. . . . No
other comedian could do as much with the dead
pan. . . . When he ran from a cop his transitions
from accelerating walk to easy jogtrot to brisk can-
ter to headlong gallop to flogged-piston sprint—
always floating, above this frenzy, the untroubled,
untouchable face—were as distinct and as soberly
in order as an automatic gear shift."

■ **610.** Simone de Beauvoir: "[The actress] is neither per-
verse not immoral, and that is why morality does
not have a chance with her. She professes great ad-
miration for James Dean. . . . At the age of eighteen
she thought that mice laid eggs. Garbo's visage

had a kind of emptiness into which anything could be projected—nothing can be read into [the actress's] face. She is alone on the screen as the strip-tease artist is alone on the stage. She offers herself directly to each spectator. But the offer is deceptive, for as the spectators watch her, they are fully aware that this beautiful young woman is famous, rich, adulated, and completely inaccessible. It is not surprising that they take her for a slut and that they take revenge on her by running her down."

■ **611.** Kenneth Tynan: "His physical presence . . . is overwhelming. He has the sauntering bulk of a fastidious yet insatiable glutton. [The actor] is perilously fat, having taken none but the slightest exercise since the time, thirty years ago, when he leapt to challenge the bulls at every village *corrida* within striking distance of Seville. Jean Cocteau rightly called him 'a giant with the face of a child,' adding that he was also 'an active loafer, a wise madman, a solitude surrounded by humanity.' Watch him in repose at a bullfight, lonely in the crowd, his brow contracted above the vast tanned jowls and his eyes bulging with reproach; into such a frame, one feels, the soul of the last American bison might easily migrate. From the pursed lips a tremendous cigar protrudes, and the chin is grimly outthrust; yet in all this dignity there is somehow an element of dimpled mischief. Beneath the swelling forehead a schoolboy winks, and can be readily coaxed into chuckling. [The actor] amused is an engulfing spectacle, as irresistible as Niagara."

■ **612.** Howard Hughes: "There are two good reasons why men will go to see her."

613. Peter Bogdanovich: "There is a splendid moment in [the film]—which features I think [the actor's] most endearing performance—when [he] walks down the steps of the sheriff's office and toward some men who are riding up to meet him. Hawks frames the shot from behind—[the actor] striding slowly, casually away from the camera in that slightly rocking graceful way of his—and the image is held for quite a long while as if to give us plenty of time to enjoy the sight: a classic, familiar figure—unmistakable from any angle—moving across a world of illusion he has more than conquered."

☆ ☆ ☆

■ **614.** What well-known Hollywood producer was as famous for his malapropisms as for his movies? Examples of the former: "Include me out," "The trouble with these directors is they're always biting the hand that lays the golden egg," "I read part of it all the way through," "He treats me like dirt under my feet," "You just don't realize what life is all about until you have found yourself lying on the brink of a great abscess," "When I see the pictures that play in that theater, it makes my hair stand on the edge of my seat," "His verbal contract is worth more than the paper it's written on," and "The next time I send a fool for something, I'll go myself."

■ **615.** Name the film—a stylish thriller, and more—that begins with Nicholas Ray singing Woody Guthrie's "Hard Travelin' " and ends with Dennis Hopper singing Bob Dylan's "I Pity the Poor Immigrant." Included in the case are six other directors. Name as many as you can.

■ **616.** Born in rural Minnesota, this blonde ex-fashion model—and mother to a current star—starred in only a handful of movies, but the first two were directed by Alfred Hitchcock (who made a much-talked-about pass at her) and the third by Charlie Chaplin. After that, nothing much. Name the actress and her daughter.

■ **617.** He acted in D. W. Griffith's *The Mother and the Law* and was an assistant director on Griffith's *Intolerance* but will undoubtedly be best remembered as the director of a bizarre movie, made in 1932, that boasted a cast comprised of dwarfs, Siamese twins, a quadruple amputee, and several microcephalics. Name the man and the movie.

■ **618.** Name the leading man, a sleepy-eyed tough guy, to whom Howard Hughes said: "You're like a pay toilet. You don't give a shit for nothing.

P O S T E R   A D   L I N E S

Name the films being advertised:

■ **619.** "There was a guy named McCrea
Who married Claudette one fine day.
She sampled his kisses and said,
'Dear, if this is
Your best then I'm going away.'
So Claudette up and took a big chance
She said, 'Florida's great for romance.'
On the train, this cute missa
Stepped right on the kisser
Of the richest young tightwad in pants."

■ **620.** "Joan the glamorous! Joan the gunfighter! She's fire and steel in her greatest role—as she faces her strangest and most exciting adventure!"

621. "These are the armies of the night! They are 100,000 strong. They outnumber the cops five to one. They could run New York City."

622. "He'll put you in a dither with his zither."

623. "A man went looking for America. And couldn't find it anywhere . . ."

624. "You are cordially invited to George and Martha's for an evening of fun and games . . ."

625. "David Cronenberg and William S. Burroughs invite you to lunch."

626. "Lots of guys swing with a call girl like Bree. One guy just wants to kill her."

627. "Being the adventures of a young man whose principal interests are rape, ultra-violence, and Beethoven."

628. "The hot-line suspense comedy."

629. "Forged by a god. Foretold by a wizard. Found by a king."

630. "This was the 85th day he went out. . . . This was the day all Hell and Heaven and Hemingway would break loose . . ."

QUIZ EIGHT

☆ ☆

M E M O R A B L E   L I N E S

Name the films in which the following lines appear as well as the actors who spoke them:

■ **631.** "God, I hate when them bastards put their hands on you. I tell you, sometimes, sometimes when I take a look at you, I just, I just keep looking and a-looking so I want to feel your little body up against me so bad I think I'm going to bust. I keep trying to tell you in a lot of different ways. If just one time you could be sweet without no money around, I think I could . . . well, I'll tell you something, I got poetry in me. I *do*! I got poetry in me. But I ain't going to put it down on paper. I ain't no educated man. I got sense enough not to try. Can't never say nothing to you. If you just one time let me run the show, I'd. . . . I'm just freezing my soul, that's what you're doing, freezing my soul."

■ **632.** "It was here. The battlefield was here. The Carthaginians defending the city were attacked by three Roman legions. The Carthaginians were

183

proud and brave but they couldn't hold and they were massacred. Arab women stripped them of their tunics and their swords and their lances. The soldiers lay naked in the sun. Two thousand years ago. I was here."

■ **633.** FIRST ACTOR: "Damn that Deke Thornton to hell!"
SECOND ACTOR: "What would you do in his place? He gave his word."
FIRST ACTOR: "Gave his word to a railroad."
SECOND ACTOR: "It's his *word!*"
FIRST ACTOR: "That ain't what counts. It's *who* you give it *to!*"

■ **634.** "Hanging's any man's business that's around.'

■ **635.** "And you are Sir Alfred de Carter! How I've looked forward to this moment, Sir Alfred! I was at your maiden concert in this country—your *debut.* . . . People said, What do you want to hear that Limey for? What does he know about music? It takes an Italian or a Russian or a Dutchman to bring it out good. But something inside of me said, Give the Limey a chance. And I did . . . and am I glad I did! That hunch has paid off in golden dividends. I've never missed one of your concerts— within the metropolitan area, of course. I'm no millionaire and can't afford to travel around the country after you to South Dakota and places like that. Here's to the world's greatest living conductor! The way you handle Handel! Sir Alfred, for me, there's you up here, and then there's *nobody*— no second, no third. . . . And your Delius—delirious! . . . I live for music!"

S C R E E N W R I T E R S   O N   F I L M

Identify the screenwriters doing the talking:

■ **636.** "I woke up in Hollywood no longer my egotistic, certain self but a mixture of Ernest [Hemingway] in fine clothes and Gerald [Murphy] with a career—and Charlie MacArthur with a past. Anybody that could make me believe that was precious to me."

■ **637.** "He made me do something that had never occurred to me before—but something I've practiced ever since: write out complete biographies of every character in the picture. Where born, educated, politics, drinking habits (if any), quirks. You take your character from his childhood and write out all the salient events in his life leading up to the moment the picture finds him—or her. The advantages are tremendous, because having thought a character out this way, his actions, his speech are thereafter compulsory; you know how he'll react to any given situation. This is in marked contrast to the usual thinking where a character is described as an 'Alan Ladd Type' or 'a sort of Humphrey Bogart guy,' or a 'Gilda character.' None of this for Ford."

■ **638.** "In a novel a hero can lay ten girls and marry a virgin for a finish. In a movie this is not allowed. The hero, as well as the heroine, has to be a virgin. The villain can lay anybody he wants, have as much fun as he wants cheating and stealing, getting rich and whipping the servants. But you have to shoot him in the end. When he falls with a bullet in his forehead, it is advisable that he clutch at the Gobelin tapestry on the library wall and bring it down over his head like a symbolic shroud. Also, covered by a tapestry, the actor does not have to hold his breath while he is being photographed as a dead man."

■ **639.** "Since it has occurred to the producers that women are 'in,' I've been offered lots of projects having to do with swingers, nuns who have left the church for carnal love, abortions, lesbians, and stories that can only be described as dramatizations of manuals of sexual techniques."

■ **640.** "Most writers pretended to despise Hollywood. I found that I adored it. . . . It was still the wild untamed territory of Before-Sound, and before the cultural pretentiousness and social· snobbery which were to come. There were still living vestiges of the days of Mabel Normand and the Keystone cops, of Francis X. Bushman and Pearl White, of John Bunny and Theda Bara. I was in Wonderland. . . . This was, of course, not a very intelligent feeling for a dedicated writer to have. but I didn't any longer have a standard for myself and my work by which I could judge and reject Hollywood. Ernest Hemingway knew what he wanted to do. So did John Dos Passos and Scott Fitzgerald. I was depending on the Oracle to speak."

☆ ☆ ☆

■ **641.** In his youth, he concocted a successful "kiss-proof" lipstick. One of Hollywood's greatest comedy writer-directors, he posited eleven rules for box-office success.

1. A pretty girl is better than an ugly one.

2. A leg is better than an arm.
3. A bedroom is better than a living room
4. An arrival is better than a departure.
5. A birth is better than a death.
6. A chase is better than a chat.
7. A dog is better than a landscape.
8. A kitten is better than a dog.
9. A baby is better than a kitten.
10. A kiss is better than a baby.
11. A pratfall is better than anything.

Name him.

■ **642.** In the modernistic Paris that Jacques Tati had built as the set for his masterpiece, *Play Time*, he had heating systems installed in the buildings even though they weren't needed and had nothing to do with the film. As well, many of the cars parked along the streets and a number of American tourists on a bus were blown-up photographs. True or false?

■ **643.** Match the unjustly neglected film in Column A with the commentary on it in Column B:

COLUMN A

1 William Fraker's *Monte Walsh*

2 Preston Sturges's *Unfaithfully Yours*

COLUMN B

a Real—or, at least, almost real—cowboys from the author of *Shane*. At the end of a cowboy's life, there's not even Catherine's ashes to scatter.

b *Local Hero*-ine meets *The Quiet Man* in Scotland. The best sea storm ever.

3 Michael Powell's and Emeric Pressburger's *I Know Where I'm Going!*

4 Robert Mulligan's *The Stalking Moon*

c *The Searchers* starring Freddy. The night *he* came home!—"he" being a particularly ferocious Indian.

d Soaring romance, sweeping poetry, plummeting pratfalls, a pirouette of a plot. Symphony scenes that are both thrilling and thrillers.

■ **644.** Known for his unremitting realism, Erich von Stroheim, while shooting *The Wedding March*, had a thousand extras—they were playing aristocrats at the court of Emperor Franz Josef—garbed in monogrammed silk underwear even though the underwear would never be seen on the screen. True or false?

■ **645.** Match the actors or actresses and films in Column A with the original choices for the roles in Column B:

COLUMN A

1 Paul Newman in Robert Rossen's *The Hustler*
2 Judy Garland in Victor Fleming's *The Wizard of Oz*
3 Faye Dunaway in Roman Polanski's *Chinatown*
4 Maruschka Detmers in Jean-Luc Godard's *First Name: Carmen*
5 Robert Duvall in Francis Coppola's *Apocalypse Now*

COLUMN B

a Kirk Douglas

b Elizabeth Taylor

c Spencer Tracy

d Lana Turner

e Claudette Colbert

6 Linda Darnell in Otto
  Preminger's *Forever Amber*
7 Montgomery Clift in Fred
  Zinnemann's *From Here
  to Eternity*
8 Edward G. Robinson in
  Norman Jewison's *The
  Cincinnati Kid*
9 Rock Hudson in John
  Frankenheimer's *Seconds*
10 Shirley MacLaine in Billy
  Wilder's *Irma La Douce*
11 Deborah Kerr in Fred
  Zinnemann's *From Here
  to Eternity*
12 Bette Davis in Joseph L
  Mankiewicz's *All About Eve*

f Deanna Durbin

g Isabelle Adjani

h Gene Hackman

i Montgomery Clift

j Jane Fonda

k Joan Crawford

l John Derek

■ **646.** Norman Rockwell painted the poster illustration for Orson Welles's *The Magnificent Ambersons*. True or false?

■ **647.** Match the unjustly neglected film in Column A with the commentary on it in Column B:

COLUMN A

1 Sam Fuller's *Park
Row*

2 Larry Yust's
Homebodies

COLUMN B

a Pygmalion plus model show up in Hollywood disguised as Joe Sternberg and Marlene. The plot boils but, oh, what a lovely smell.

b Aging lion-as-kidnapper only wants the money. Boon companion rapes and murders the little girl anyway. Lion becomes wild one again and machine-guns him dead. Or was it all a dream?

3 Robert Aldrich's *The Legend of Lylah Clare*

c Up the river with Eisenstein. the Montage of Attractions meets the Heart of Darkness.

4 Richard Sarafian's *Vanishing Point*

d Naïf meets older man—is it love? He ruins himself over her, she becomes a movie star, gives suicide a try, and never comes out of the ether. Neither will you.

5 Hubert Cornfield's *The Night of the Following Day*

e Crusading little newspaper vs. the big combo. Horace Greeley looks on, Brodie dives off the Brooklyn Bridge, truth and love win out.

6 Max Ophuls's *La signora di tutti*

f Being chased, chasing the horizon, chasing himself, he speeds his Charger across the desert to the California line and a bulldozer named death.

7 Carol Reed's *Outcast of the Island*

g You're old, getting evicted, and live in Cincinnati; no wonder you start killing people.

■ **648.** During hard times, this internationally famous director worked at the Museum of Modern Art on an anti-Nazi film (he was fired), dubbed films for Warner Brothers in the forties, and lost out to Robert Florey as the director of a little horror number called *The Beast With Five Fingers*. Fortunately, he made quite a career comeback—beginning in Mexico. Name the director.

P O S T E R   A D   L I N E S

Name the films being advertised:

■ **649.** "Every man's past is his own secret in the Foreign Legion—but this woman makes the past live "

■ **650.** "135 women—with men on their minds!"

■ **651.** "A kinky movie with a full head of steam."

■ **652.** "The extraordinary Mexican-Wagnerian melodrama adapted from the classic by Emily Brontë."

■ **653.** "A terrifyingly tasteful comedy for adults who can count."

■ **654.** "Well, any scientist who makes a girl like this can't be all bad."

■ **655.** "100 years ago they were called Samurai."

QUIZ EIGHT

MEMORABLE LINES

Name the films in which the following lines appear as well as the actors who spoke them:

- **656.** "Someday a car will pick me up that I never thumbed."

- **657.** "Everything has been said. At least as long as words don't change their meanings and meanings their words. It is quite obvious that someone who usually lives at the limit of suffering requires a different form of religion than a person who normally lives securely. Nothing existed here before us. No one. We are completely alone. We are uniquely, dreadfully alone. The meaning of words and expressions can no longer be grasped. An isolated word or an isolated detail in a drawing can be understood. But the meaning of the whole escapes us. Once we know the number 1, we believe we know the number 2, because 1 plus 1 equals 2. We forget that, first, we must know the meaning of *plus*."

■ **658.** "It seems to me that my coming into the world was a terrible fall."

■ **659.** "Ah! He ain't my leader. I got my own way of taking banks. I come in shooting. I kill everyone in sight. I grab the dough. Very easy. Works very well. You don't like it, you get somebody else."

■ **660.** "Didn't you hear about me, Gabe? If I'd been a ranch, they would have named me the Bar Nothing."

■ **661.** "I work all week and then on Sundays I watch other people ride the merry-go-round."

■ **662.** "I have already chosen my grave under a mulberry tree. Yesterday I ordered the stone and decided on the inscription. Just two words. *Amor Omnia.* I told the gardener there is only to be grass on the grave and in the springtime anemones. If you pass by one day, pick an anemone and think of me. Take it as a word of love, a love I thought but never spoke. . . . One day your visit will be a memory like all the memories I keep and cherish. I feel I'm staring into a fire about to be extinguished."

■ **663.** "I made a million plans looking at this wallpaper."

S C R E E N W R I T E R S   O N   F I L M

Identify the screenwriters doing the talking:

■ **664.** "Writing is easy: all you do is sit staring at the blank sheet of paper until the drops of blood form on your forehead."

■ **665.** "Forty years ago, when John Huston had taken the plunge and become a director, I asked him why. 'Because,' he replied, 'the director gets to fuck the star.' Whether this directorial *droit du seigneur* exists or not is unimportant; what is important is that the public, and possibly the critics, *believe* that it exists, thus subtly lending further credence to the myth of the director as procreator, begetter, author. If any devotee of the Auteur Theory happens to be reading this, I should like to ask him a question: who was the Auteur of *How Green Was My Valley*? Since according to the rules only directors can be Auteurs, we can immediately rule out Richard Llewellyn, Darryl Zanuck, and Philip Dunne. The question is which director? Was it Willy Wyler, who worked with me for many weeks on the script, on the casting and the set construction, in fact did everything a director does but actually shoot the picture? Or was it Jack Ford, who with only a few minor changes, faithfully and brilliantly shot the script. I don't think anyone can answer the question because the entire premise of the theory is false. I have often wondered what *How Green Was My Valley* would have been like had Wyler directed it instead of Ford. There would have been differences, of course: completely different camera angles, different emphases, different shadings in the performances. But these differences wouldn't have been much greater than the differences you might detect if you listened to Jascha Heifetz play Beethoven's Violin Concerto and then to David Oistrakh or Yehudi Menuhin play the same work. In all the performing arts, individual interpretation is important, but never as important as the basic material."

■ **666.** "The noble piety of Hollywood folks, as they immersed themselves in the plight of the migratory workers and the like, was pretty comical. One couldn't fault them for their social conscience, but when you saw the English country houses they dwelt in, the hundred-thousand-dollar *estancias*, and the Cadillacs they drove to the protest meetings, it was to laugh."

■ **667.** "James Cain was weary of the rip-off by the producers. They paid a writer but once for his material, but could use it again and again. Cain came to the Screen Writers Guild with a plan to put an end to this malpractice. His proposal was modeled after the very successful organization of the songwriters. Under ASCAP rules no song ... could be used without paying the authors a fee for each performance. It put an end to free use of their material and changed the miserable economic status of the membership overnight. James Cain was a politically conservative man, and there was no way to attack this plan by red-baiting him. But when I, as vice-president of the Guild, joined in its advocacy, the red-baiters had a target. Suddenly I was publicized as the author of Cain's proposal. Cain, easily seduced, apparently believed the canards of those who sought to discredit his plan, and in 1948 angrily denounced me, Ring Lardner, and Gordon Kahn as stealing his plan and of being loyal first to the Communist Party and only then to the Screen Writers Guild."

■ **668.** "I feel if a writer becomes cynical about his work in films, he should be doing something else. I've never looked down on the film medium—or even on Hollywood in spite of its well-advertised inani-

ties and its haphazard mass-production system.
Writing a screenplay ... is only part of a writer's
function; struggling to preserve its values is the
other part. If he cares enough, he'll do it."

☆ ☆ ☆

■ **669.** In the early fifties, when Charlie Chaplin said,
"This is the greatest movie ever made about
America," he was talking about (a) his own *A King
in New York* (b) *A Place in the Sun*, George Stevens's
remake of Theodore Dreiser's *An American Tragedy*
(c) Howard Hawks's *Red River* (d) Frank Capra's
It's a Wonderful Life (e) Henry King's *Twelve O'Clock
High*?

■ **670.** Name the loose remake of Vittorio De Sica's *The
Bicycle Thief* in which a dog plays the little boy's—
Enzo Staiola's—part.

■ **671.** With a single exception, Robert Burks was Alfred
Hitchcock's cinematographer from *Strangers on a
Train* (1951) through *Marnie* (1964). Name the
movie on which Burks didn't work and the reason
why.

■ **672.** The first woman ever nominated for an Oscar as
Best Director was (a) Lillian Gish for *Remodeling
Her Husband* (1920), (b) Dorothy Arzner for *The
Bride Wore Red* (1937), (c) Ida Lupino for *The Hitch-
hiker* (1953), (d) Marguerite Duras for *Destroy She
Said* (1969), (e) Lina Wertmuller for *Seven Beauties*
(1976)?

■ **673.** Before each of the characters in Column A died,
he or she delivered his or her final words to the
world in Column B. Match them:

COLUMN A	COLUMN B
1 José Ferrer in Otto Preminger's *Whirlpool*	**a** "Give us a kiss.'
2 Donald Pleasance in John Sturges's *The Great Escape*	**b** "I'm afraid you're right, tonight I was a bit stupid."
3 Robert Mitchum in Nicholas Ray's *The Lusty Men*	**c** "It's a bad joke without a punch line."
4 Ray Danton in Budd Boetticher's *The Rise and Fall of Legs Diamond*	**d** "Thank you for getting me out."
5 Marie Gomez in Richard Brooks's *The Professionals*	**e** "You can't kill me."
6 Marie Windsor in Stanley Kubrick's *The Killing*	**f** "Guys like me last forever."

■ **674.** This early French sound film was made for a small company whose financing dried up in mid-production, forcing the director to release it even though the picture made little sense. Nevertheless, Jean-Luc Godard opined that the picture was "the only great French thriller or rather the greatest French adventure film of all." Name the movie and the director.

■ **675.** Match the films in Column A (all remakes) with those in Column B (the original versions):

COLUMN A	COLUMN B
1 Stuart Heisler's *I Died a Thousand Times*	**a** Robert Montgomery's *Ride the Pink Horse*
2 Robert Sparr's *Once You Kiss a Stranger*	**b** Henry Hathaway's *Kiss of Death*

3 Gordon Douglas's *The Fiend Who Walked the West*

4 Eddie Davis's *Color Me Dead*

5 Don Siegel's *The Hanged Man*

6 Robert D. Webb's *The Capetown Affair*

7 Harry Keller's *Step Down to Terror*

8 William Dieterle's *Satan Met a Lady*

9 Taylor Hackford's *Against All Odds*

10 George Armitage's *Hit Man*

11 Robert Alan Arthur's *The Lost Man*

12 Louis Malle's *Crackers*

c Raoul Walsh's *High Sierra*

d Mario Monicelli's *Big Deal on Madonna Street*

e Sam Fuller's *Pickup on South Street*

f Mike Hodges's *Get Carter*

g Carol Reed's *Odd Man Out*

h Rudolph Maté's *D.O.A.*

i Alfred Hitchcock's *Strangers on a Train*

j Roy Del Ruth's *The Maltese Falcon*

k Alfred Hitchcock's *Shadow of a Doubt*

l Jacques Tourneur's *Out of the Past*

■ **676.** Arguably, the classiest double entendre in movies:

> ACTOR: "All I do is wave a little wand a little, and out comes the music."
>
> ACTRESS: "A little magic wand, darling, dipped in a little stardust."

Name the actor, the actress, and the film.

■ **677.** This country was the first to recognize the movies as an art form and not just a novelty item for the masses. Yet, in 1930, its entire film industry produced only nine pictures because the bottom had dropped out of its foreign market, a result of the inroads made around the world by the Hollywood product. The country was (a) Italy (b) Germany (c) France (d) Sweden (e) Japan?

■ **678.** In Carol Reed's 1949 film, *The Third Man*, the villainous Orson Welles uses the sewer system of Vienna as a means of traveling undetected through the city. Name the American crime movie, released in either late 1948 or early 1949 (accounts differ), in which a criminal uses the Los Angeles sewer system as a means of traveling undetected through the city. (This is coincidence, not theft.)

D I R E C T O R S   o n   F I L M

Identify the directors doing the talking:

■ **679.** "All you ever hear in a studio are these three phrases: 'Let's get down to work,' 'There isn't any money,' and 'You don't love me anymore.' "

■ **680.** "I made mistakes in drama. I thought drama was when actors cried. But drama is when the audience cries."

■ **681.** "If we were living in a period of high civilization, like the twelfth century, and not in our own, dubbers would be burned in the public squares for having committed the sin of asserting that one body can have several souls."

■ **682.** "I stoutly maintain that a good film must reflect the country of its origin."

■ **683.** "If Christ hadn't risen, there would have been no story."

CINEMATOGRAPHERS ON FILM

Identify the cinematographers doing the talking:

■ **684.** "A cameraman is often the chief in a film. His lighting can be the main factor in its success. Very few directors know anything about the uses of light. Von Sternberg knew a great deal, but even he couldn't see the necessity for the balance of light and shadow in a shot. You can follow my style like a thread through many directors' films. Ever since I began, Rembrandt has been my favorite artist. I've always used his technique of north light—of having my main source of light on a set coming from the north. And of course I've always followed Rembrandt in my fondness for low key. I like to highlight significant detail, and I have been able to do this in spite of a great variety of directors."

■ **685.** "The basic principle I have had in making pictures was to make them look like real life, and them *emphasize the visuals slightly*. I always tried to avoid a monotonous succession of beautiful shots. I'd have a drab one in between. And I always liked simple effects. In *The Birth of a Nation* Billy Bitzer had no proper lights at one stage, so for a street scene he just used one lousy sun arc right up at the back of the set, and it made a beautiful pattern. That's the way to do it: improvise, invent."

■ **686.** "Even though a thing might be technically wrong, to me that wrong thing can be *dramatically* right. To hell with this 'academic' approach! You must *distort* color, play around with it, make it work for you, intentionally throw it off balance. There are times when nature is dull: change it. I've always maintained that color photography should not be naturalistic "

■ **687.** "I have a basic approach that goes on from film to film: to make all the sources of light absolutely naturalistic. If you are in a room and the scene is taking place at a certain time of day, try to find out where the light would come from, and follow that, don't impose an artificial style In color that's difficult to control. You can fake a 'true' look in the color laboratory but then it becomes an achievement of chemistry, not cinematography."

■ **688.** "I began making experimental films. B. P. Schulberg of Paramount finally saw them and sent for me. He signed me up in 1932. I was broke; I had squandered my money on poor, starving girls, whisky, and so on. Zanuck gave me outright freedom at 20th. There I developed my technique of using the absolute minimum lights on a set. I'd always say, 'God was a great photographer. He'd only gotten one light.' "

P O S T E R   A D   L I N E S

Name the films being advertised:

■ **689.** "A romance of love and potatoes."

■ **690.** "Children of ice and darkness. ... They are the lurking, unseen evil you dare not face alone!"

■ **691.** "We've got nothing to hide..."

■ **692.** "One man . . three women ... one night!"

■ **693.** "Sensational and startling 'hold up' of the 'Gold Express' by famous Western outlaws."

694. "Whether you live in a small town the way they do, or in a city, maybe this is happening to you right now ... maybe (if you're older) you remember ... when suddenly the kissing isn't a kid's game anymore, suddenly it's wide-eyed, scary, and dangerous."

695. "For one moment they held history in their hands. With one terrible blow, they made it."

696. "A robot and a man ... hold the world spellbound with new and startling powers from another planet!"

697. "God-less, love-less, heartless, he fought his brutal way up to the pinnacle of power, only to be challenged by a frail woman."

698. "A picture that goes beyond what men think about—because no man ever thought about it in quite this way!"

699. "One brother wanted her for what she was—the other for what she could be!"

700. "As boys, they made a pact to share their fortunes, their loves, their lives. As men, they shared a dream to rise from poverty to power. Forging an empire built on greed, violence, and betrayal, their dream would end as a mystery that refused to die."

701. "The world as they knew it was slipping away. Time was running out for the human race. And there was nothing to hold on to—except each other!"

QUIZ ONE

The Answers

1. If your answer was Orson Welles in *Citizen Kane*, you're only half right. The line was actually spoken by George Coulouris, quoting a letter written to him by Kane/Welles.
2. Humphrey Bogart to Dooley Wilson about Ingrid Bergman in Michael Curtiz's *Casablanca*.
3. Jimmy Stewart and Kim Novak in Alfred Hitchcock's *Vertigo*.
4. Robert Duvall in Francis Coppola's *Apocalypse Now*.
5. Charlie Chaplin in Chaplin's *Limelight*.
6. In Orson Welles's *Citizen Kane*, Welles and Ruth Warrick play the nine-year breakfast scene on the same set in a series of dissolves, with changes in lighting, makeup, wardrobe, and props.
7.   **1** Carlo Ponti   **f** Sophia Loren
         2 Mickey Rooney   **h** Ava Gardner
         3 Vincente Minnelli   **b** Judy Garland
         4 Harold Pinter   **a** Vivien Merchant
         5 Charles Laughton   **j** Elsa Lanchester
         6 Federico Fellini   **i** Giulietta Masina

> 7 Roberto Rossellini   **l** Ingrid Bergman
> 8 Cary Grant   **c** Dyan Cannon
> 9 Blake Edwards   **d** Julie Andrews
> 10 Irving Thalberg   **e** Norma Shearer
> 11 Laurence Olivier   **g** Vivien Leigh
> 12 Brian De Palma   **k** Nancy Allen

8. Max Ophuls, who directed James Mason in *Caught* and *The Reckless Moment*.

9.
> 1 Paul Newman   **g** *Rachel, Rachel*
> 2 Marlon Brando   **f** *One-Eyed Jacks*
> 3 Dennis Hopper   **e** *Easy Rider*
> 4 Charles Laughton   **h** *The Night of the Hunter*
> 5 Laurence Olivier   **c** *Henry V*
> 6 Warren Beatty   **a** *Reds*
> 7 Clint Eastwood   **d** *Play Misty for Me*
> 8 Robert Montgomery   **i** *Lady in the Lake*
> 9 John Wayne   **b** *The Alamo*

10. Billy Wilder's *Sunset Boulevard*.
11. Alfred Hitchcock.
12. Ingmar Bergman.
13. Jean-Luc Godard.
14. Federico Fellini.
15. François Truffaut, about the final shot of *The 400 Blows*.
16. True.
17. Republic.
18.
> 1 Barbra Streisand's *Yentl*   **e** *Tootsie on the Roof*
> 2 Jacques Rivette's *Paris Belongs to Us*   **c** *Marienbad Belongs to Us*
> 3 King Vidor's *Duel in the Sun*   **f** *Lust in the Dust*
> 4 Francis Coppola's *One From the Heart*   **b** *One From the Computer*
> 5 W S Van Dyke's *I Take this Woman*   **a** *I Retake This Woman*

6 Warren Beatty's   **g** *Commie Dearest*
Reds

7 Clint Eastwood's   **d** *Dirty Harriet*
Sudden Impact

19. Mickey Spillane played Mike Hammer in Roy Rowland's *The Girl Hunters*.
20. Orson Welles to Carol Reed about the role of Harry Lime in Reed's *The Third Man*. The film's climactic chase sequences were shot in the Vienna sewers.
21. *Bonnie and Clyde* (Arthur Penn).
22. *The Great Dictator* (Charlie Chaplin).
23. *Wings of Desire* (Wim Wenders).
24. *Raise the Red Lantern* (Zhang Yimou).
25. *Tootsie* (Sydney Pollack).

QUIZ ONE

The Answers

26. Hank Worden to John Wayne and Jeffrey Hunter in John Ford's *The Searchers*.

27. Cyd Charisse in Rouben Mamoulian's *Silk Stockings*.

28. Robert Greig to Joel McCrea in Preston Sturges's *Sullivan's Travels*.

29. Humphrey Bogart to Joan Leslie in Raoul Walsh's *High Sierra*.

30. Sal Mineo to James Dean in Nicholas Ray's *Rebel Without a Cause*.

31. They are initials added later—for self-importance.

32.

1	Dudley Moore	**d**	Tuesday Weld
2	Jack Lemmon	**c**	Felicia Farr
3	Jean-Luc Godard	**k**	Anna Karina
4	Ronald Colman	**j**	Benita Hume
5	Stewart Granger	**g**	Jean Simmons
6	Vic Damone	**a**	Pier Angeli
7	Rod Steiger	**h**	Claire Bloom
8	Jack Webb	**f**	Julie London
9	Joseph Cotten	**b**	Patricia Medina

10 Garson Kanin	**l** Ruth Gordon
11 Louis Malle	**i** Candice Bergen
12 Jean-Pierre Aumont	**e** Maria Montez

33. Edmund Wilson.

34.		
	1 Elaine May	**h** *A New Leaf*
	2 Peter Fonda	**a** *The Hired Hand*
	3 Albert Finney	**b** *Charlie Bubbles*
	4 Jeanne Moreau	**f** *La Lumière*
	5 Anna Karina	**d** *Vivre Ensemble*
	6 Laurence Harvey	**e** *The Ceremony*
	7 Jack Lemmon	**g** *Kotch*
	8 James Caan	**c** *Hide in Plain Sight*

35. Leslie Howard.

36. Jean Renoir.

37. Robert Bresson.

38. Fritz Lang.

39. John Ford.

40. Jean-Luc Godard.

41. James Dean, nominated for Elia Kazan's production of John Steinbeck's *East of Eden* and George Stevens's production of Edna Ferber's *Giant*. He was killed in a car crash on September 30, 1955, shortly after completing his role in the latter.

42. If you answered either Herman J. Mankiewicz or Nunnally Johnson, you're right. Both men have been credited with the line.

43. Alan (or Allen) Smithee is the name to which the Directors Guild of America credits a film—on the screen—when the actual director has had his name removed from the production. *Death of a Gunfighter* was codirected by Don Siegel and *Let's Get Harry* was directed by Stuart Rosenberg, but many of the Smithees are hardly household names even among cinéphiles. Even so, Alan Smithee is proof indeed that there are people of principle in the film industry: otherwise why would the director of *The Shrimp on the Barbie* (with Cheech Marin) have had his name stricken from the credits if not for the inter ference of uncultured ignoramuses trying to com promise his artistic integrity?

44. False. According to Hawks, Capone liked *Scarface* so much he had his own print.

45. Jean Renoir's *La Règle du jeu*. Bergman goes on to say: "Renoir is a very overrated director. He has made only one good picture, *La Bête humaine*"

46. *The Legend of Lylah Clare* (Robert Aldrich).

47. *The Searchers* (John Ford).

48. *Network* (Sidney Lumet; script by Paddy Chayefsky).

49. *Ninotchka* (Ernst Lubitsch).

50. *Young Mr. Lincoln* (John Ford).

The Answers

- **51.** Orson Welles in Welles's *Touch of Evil*.
- **52.** John Garfield about Thomas Gomez in Abraham Polonsky's *Force of Evil*.
- **53.** Ben Gazzara to Peter Bogdanovich in Bogdanovich's *Saint Jack*.
- **54.** Rutger Hauer to Harrison Ford in Ridley Scott's *Blade Runner*.
- **55.** Eddie Constantine in Jean-Luc Godard's *Alphaville*.
- **56.** Buster Keaton.
- **57.**

1	Anthony Mann	**c**	Sarita Montiel
2	William Holden	**e**	Brenda Marshall
3	Don Siegel	**d**	Viveca Lindfors
4	Richard Brooks	**b**	Jean Simmons
5	Rudy Vallee	**g**	Jane Greer
6	William Friedkin	**a**	Jeanne Moreau
7	Jean-Pierre Aumont	**i**	Marisa Pavan
8	Jed Harris	**k**	Ruth Gordon
9	Sean Connery	**j**	Diane Cilento
10	Jean-Luc Godard	**h**	Anne Wiazemsky
11	Albert Finney	**f**	Anouk Aimée

58. Ben Hecht.

59.

1 Mickey Rooney		**f**	*My True Story*
2 Dick Powell		**b**	*Split Second*
3 Ralph Richardson		**i**	*Home at Seven*
4 Walter Matthau		**g**	*Gangster Story*
5 Burt Lancaster		**c**	*The Kentuckian*
6 Frank Sinatra		**h**	*None But the Brave*
7 Kirk Douglas		**a**	*Posse*
8 Toshiro Mifune		**j**	*The Legacy of the Five Hundred Thousand*
9 Lillian Gish		**e**	*Remodeling Her Husband*
10 Anthony Quinn		**d**	*The Buccaneer* (1958)

60. Ronald Reagan in Don Siegel's *The Killers*.

61. François Truffaut.

62. René Clair.

63. Robert Bresson.

64. Douglas Sirk.

65. Erich von Stroheim about *The Merry Widow*.

66. French cinéaste Nino Frank. *Série noire. Black Mask.*

67. Sam Fuller.

68. None of these directors was ever voted Best Director of the year by the Academy of Motion Picture Arts and Sciences, though several were awarded special Oscars for career achievement.

69. Billy Wilder. The film was *Sunset Boulevard*.

70. Mark Robson's *The Seventh Victim* was produced by Val Lewton, the *auteur* of low-budget horror films such as *Cat People* and *I Walked With a Zombie* for RKO in the forties. In *The Seventh Victim*, Kim Hunter is shown taking a shower while a shadowy figure, moving ominously closer and closer, is seen through the plastic shower curtain.

71. *Stagecoach* (John Ford).

72. *The Killing* (Stanley Kubrick).

- **73.** *Casablanca* (Michael Curtiz).
- **74.** *Dirty Harry* (Don Siegel).
- **75.** *The Beautiful Blonde From Bashful Bend* (Preston Sturges).

Quiz Two

The Answers

■ **76.** Gloria Swanson in Billy Wilder's *Sunset Boulevard*.

■ **77.** Burt Lancaster to Robert Joy in Louis Malle's *Atlantic City*.

■ **78.** Walter Huston to a group of Tampico down-and-outers, which includes Humphrey Bogart and Tim Holt, in John Huston's *The Treasure of the Sierra Madre*.

■ **79.** Cary Grant to Eva Marie Saint in Alfred Hitchcock's *North by Northwest*.

■ **80.** Max von Sydow in Ingmar Bergman's *The Seventh Seal*.

■ **81.** Josef von Sternberg's *Underworld* (1927).

■ **82.** Tim Holt, son of Jack, sister of Jennifer. Who can forget him as George Amberson Minafer in Orson Welles's production of *The Magnificent Ambersons* and as Curtin in *The Treasure of the Sierra Madre*?

■ **83.**
1	John Ford	**h**	Frank S. Nugent
2	Howard Hawks	**j**	William Faulkner
3	Vittorio De Sica	**i**	Cesare Zavattini
4	Billy Wilder	**g**	I. A L. Diamond

5	Carol Reed	**a**	Graham Greene
6	David Lean	**d**	Robert Bolt
7	Elia Kazan	**e**	Budd Schulberg
8	Marcel Carné	**c**	Jacques Prévert
9	Alain Resnais	**f**	Alain Robbe-Grillet
10	Joseph Losey	**b**	Harold Pinter

■ **84.** Betty Boop.

■ **85.** Alexander Mackendrick's *Sweet Smell of Success*, in which Burt Lancaster plays a power-mad Walter Winchell type and Tony Curtis a power-craving press agent. Susan Harrison and Martin Milner are the young lovers.

■ **86.** **1 d** Jean-Paul Belmondo was the original choice for the Oskar Werner role in François Truffaut's *Fahrenheit 451*.

2 e Ronald Reagan was the original choice for the Humphrey Bogart role in Michael Curtiz's *Casablanca*.

3 h Brigitte Bardot was the original choice for the Isabelle Huppert role in Joseph Losey's *The Trout*.

4 f Marlon Brando was the original choice for the Kirk Douglas role in Elia Kazan's *The Arrangement*.

5 b Montgomery Clift was the original choice for the James Dean role in Elia Kazan's production of John Steinbeck's *East of Eden*.

6 a Laurence Olivier was the original choice for the James Mason role in George Cukor's *A Star Is Born*.

7 c Ava Gardner was the original choice for the Doris Day role in Charles Vidor's *Love Me or Leave Me*.

8 g Ingrid Bergman was the original choice for the Alida Valli role in Luchino Visconti's *Senso*.

■ **87.** Alfred Hitchcock, who was directing *The Paradine Case* at the time.

■ **88.** **1 e** Howard Hawks's *His Girl Friday* was a remake of Lewis Milestone's production of Ben Hecht's and Charles MacArthur's play *The Front Page*.

2 g John Ford's *Mogambo* was a remake of Victor Fleming's *Red Dust*.

3 h Bob Fosse's *Cabaret* was a remake of Henry Cornelius's *I Am a Camera* (based on Christopher Isherwood's book of the same name).

4 a Warren Beatty's and Buck Henry's *Heaven Can Wait* was a remake of Alexander Hall's *Here Comes Mr. Jordan*.

5 j Charles Walter's *High Society* was a remake of George Cukor's *The Philadelphia Story*.

6 b Roger Vadim's *Circle of Love* was a remake of Max Ophuls's *La Ronde*.

7 d Sidney Lumet's *The Wiz* was a remake of Victor Fleming's *The Wizard of Oz*.

8 i William Friedkin's *Sorcerer* was a remake of H. G. Clouzot's *The Wages of Fear*.

9 f Bob Fosse's *Sweet Charity* was a remake of Federico Fellini's *Nights of Cabiria*.

10 c George Marshall's *Fancy Pants* was a remake of Leo McCarey's *Ruggles of Red Gap*.

■ **89.** Metro-Goldwyn-Mayer. In its heyday, MGM had under contract Clark Gable, Greta Garbo, Norma Shearer, the Barrymores, Jean Harlow, Joan Crawford, Spencer Tracy, Robert Taylor, Jimmy Stewart, Myrna Loy, Mickey Rooney, Greer Garson, William Powell, Walter Pidgeon, and Elizabeth Taylor.

■ **90.** Kris Kristofferson in Michael Cimino's *Heaven's Gate*

- **91.** *The Wild Bunch* (Sam Peckinpah).
- **92.** *Rebel Without a Cause* (Nicholas Ray)
- **93.** *Some Like It Hot* (Billy Wilder).
- **94.** *Paths of Glory* (Stanley Kubrick).
- **95.** *Local Hero* (Bill Forsyth), a good little film despite the ungrammatical copy for the poster.
- **96.** *A Taxing Woman* (Juzo Itami).
- **97.** *The Burmese Harp* (Kon Ichikawa).
- **98.** *Big Deal on Madonna Street* (Mario Monicelli), which was remade as *Crackers* (Louis Malle).
- **99.** *Sullivan's Travels* (Preston Sturges).
- **100.** *The Roaring Twenties* (Raoul Walsh).

QUIZ TWO
☆ ☆

The Answers

101. Humphrey Bogart, trying out some lines from a script he's writing, to Gloria Grahame in Nicholas Ray's *In a Lonely Place*. After the romance has ended tragically, Grahame says, as much to herself as to the departing Bogart: "I lived a few days while you loved me. Goodbye, Dix."

102. John Barrymore to several people in Howard Hawks's production of Ben Hecht's and Charles MacArthur's play *Twentieth Century*.

103. Peter Firth to Nastassia Kinski in Roman Polanski's production of Thomas Hardy's *Tess*.

104. Thelma Ritter to Richard Kiley in Sam Fuller's *Pickup on South Street*.

105. Robert De Niro in Martin Scorsese's *Taxi Driver*.

106. John Dall, who starred in Joseph H. Lewis's *Gun Crazy* and Alfred Hitchcock's *Rope*. Dall's Best Supporting Actor nomination was for Irving Rapper's *The Corn Is Green*.

107. C. S. Forester's *The African Queen*, directed by John Huston.

■ **108.**

1 Budd Boetticher	**h** Burt Kennedy
2 Josef von Sternberg	**i** Jules Furthman
3 Mitchell Leisen	**f** Preston Sturges
4 Michael Curtiz	**b** Howard Koch
5 D W. Griffith	**g** Anita Loos
6 Frank Capra	**d** Robert Riskin
7 George Cukor	**j** Garson Kanin
8 Martin Scorsese	**c** Mardik Martin
9 Alfred Hitchcock	**e** Alma Reville
10 Fritz Lang	**a** Theda von Harbou

■ **109.** Joseph Losey's *Boom!* (based on Williams's *The Milk Train Doesn't Stop Here Any More*), in which Richard Burton plays the Angel of Death come to collect Elizabeth Taylor, a terminally ill, abusive dictator of her own private island in the Mediterranean. The picture was reviled by reviewers at the time and is still derogated today by such unreliables as Leonard Maltin. It has not been released on videotape.

■ **110.** (c) Cary Grant.

■ **111.**

    1 e Jean-Luc Godard's *Pierrot le fou* was based on Lionel White's *Obsession*.

    2 j Karel Reisz's *Who'll Stop the Rain* was based on Robert Stone's *Dog Soldiers*.

    3 c George Stevens's *A Place in the Sun* was based on Theodore Dreiser's *An American Tragedy*.

    4 i Don Siegel's *The Gun Runners* and Michael Curtiz's *The Breaking Point* were based on Ernest Hemingway's *To Have and Have Not*.

    5 b Luchino Visconti's *Ossessione* and Pierre Chenal's *Le Dernier tournant* were based on James M. Cain's *The Postman Always Rings Twice*.

6 d John Ford's *Dr. Bull* was based on James Gould Cozzens's *The Last Adam*.

7 h John Boulting's *Young Scarface* was based on Graham Greene's *Brighton Rock*.

8 f John Ford's *The Fugitive* was based on Graham Greene's *The Power and the Glory*.

9 a Jean-Luc Godard's *Contempt* was based on Albert Moravia's *A Ghost at Noon*.

10 g Douglas Sirk's *A Time to Love and a Time to Die* was based on Erich Maria Remarque's *A Time to Live and a Time to Die*.

■ **112.** Jean-Pierre Melville, who named himself after Herman Melville.

■ **113.** **1 e** A segment from Vincente Minnelli's *The Bad and the Beautiful* appears in Minnelli's *Two Weeks in Another Town*.

2 d A segment from Roger Corman's *Tomb of Ligeia* appears in Martin Scorsese's *Mean Streets*.

3 i A segment from Howard Hawks's *Red River* appears in Peter Bogdanovich's *The Last Picture Show*.

4 f A segment from Howard Hawks's *The Thing From Another World* appears in John Carpenter's *Halloween*.

5 g A segment from George Hill's *Hell Divers* appears in John Ford's *The Wings of Eagles*.

6 j A segment from Joseph H. Lewis's *Gun Crazy* appears in Jim McBride's *Breathless*.

7 a A segment from Roberto Rossellini's *Voyage in Italy* appears in Jean-Luc Godard's *Contempt*.

8 c A segment from Michael Anderson's *The Dam Busters* appears in Alan Parker's *Pink Floyd: The Wall*.

9 h A segment from Laslo Benedek's *The Wild One* appears in Kenneth Anger's *Scorpio Rising.*

10 b A segment from Fritz Lang's *Metropolis* appears in Jacques Rivette's *Paris Belongs to Us.*

114. Bella Darvi.

115. The first picture in Orson Welles's three-picture deal with RKO was *Citizen Kane.* While finishing Booth Tarkington's *The Magnificent Ambersons,* his second production, Welles supervised Norman Foster's direction of the third and last RKO picture, *Journey Into Fear,* which starred Joseph Cotten and Dolores Del Rio.

116. *Gun Crazy* (Joseph H. Lewis).

117. *Picnic* (play by William Inge; directed by Josh Logan).

118. *Monsieur Verdoux* (Charlie Chaplin).

119. *The Road Warrior* (George Miller).

120. *My Life to Live* (Jean-Luc Godard).

121. *Strangers on a Train* (Alfred Hitchcock).

122. *Scarlet Street* (Fritz Lang).

123. *Sunset Boulevard* (Billy Wilder).

124. *Targets* (Peter Bogdanovich).

125. *Sotto Sotto* (Lina Wertmuller).

QUIZ TWO

The Answers

126. Edgar Kennedy in Preston Sturges's *The Sin of Harold Diddlebock* (a.k.a. *Mad Wednesday!!!*).

127. James Mason in Carol Reed's *The Man Between*.

128. William Powell in Gregory La Cava's *My Man Godfrey*.

129. Orson Welles to Robert Arden in Welles's *Mr. Arkadin*.

130. Dudley Sutton in Ken Russell's *The Devils*.

131. True.

132. Max Nosseck's *Dillinger*.

133.
1	Ernst Lubitsch	**e**	Samson Raphaelson
2	Federico Fellini	**b**	Tullio Pinelli
3	Roberto Rossellini	**i**	Federico Fellini
4	Jean-Luc Godard	**h**	Jean-Pierre Gorin
5	Robert Aldrich	**g**	Lukas Heller
6	Claude Chabrol	**d**	Paul Gégauff
7	Roman Polanski	**a**	Gerard Brach
8	James Ivory	**j**	Ruth Prawer Jhabvala
9	Luchino Visconti	**c**	Suso Cecchi d'Amico
10	Michelangelo Antonioni	**f**	Tonino Guerra

■ **134.** Joe Pasternak.

■ **135.** (e) Frances Farmer, whom Hawks directed in *Come and Get It*. William Wyler codirected the film.

■ **136.** **1 c** Cary Grant was the original choice for the Lamberto Maggiorani role in Vittorio De Sica's *The Bicycle Thief*.

 2 d Marlon Brando was the original choice for the Farley Granger role in Luchino Visconti's *Senso*.

 3 g Albert Finney was the original choice for the Peter O'Toole role in David Lean's *Lawrence of Arabia*.

 4 f George Segal was the original choice for the Dudley Moore role in Blake Edwards's *"10."*

 5 e Frank Sinatra was the original choice for the Warren Beatty role in George Stevens's *The Only Game in Town*.

 6 a Montgomery Clift was the original choice for the William Holden role in Billy Wilder's *Sunset Boulevard*.

 7 h Robert Redford was the original choice for the Dustin Hoffman role in Mike Nichols's *The Graduate*.

 8 b José Ferrer was the original choice for the Ray Milland role in Billy Wilder's *The Lost Weekend*.

■ **137.** John Carpenter, who won for coscripting, editing, and scoring *The Resurrection of Bronco Billy*, produced by UCLA's Department of Cinema

■ **138.** **1 b** Frank Tashlin's *Rock-a-Bye Baby* was a remake of Preston Sturges's *The Miracle of Morgan's Creek*.

 2 j Robert Z. Leonard's *In the Good Old Summertime* was a remake of Ernest Lubitsch's *The Shop Around the Corner*.

 3 i George Cukor's *Rich and Famous* was a

remake of Vincent Sherman's *Old Acquaintance*.

4 g Howard Hawks's *A Song Is Born* was a remake of Hawks's *Ball of Fire*.

5 c John Cromwell's *Algiers* was a remake of Julien Duvivier's *Pépé le Moko*.

6 d Frank Capra's *Pocketful of Miracles* was a remake of Capra's *Lady for a Day*.

7 e Charles Marquis Warren's *Hellgate* was a remake of John Ford's *The Prisoner of Shark Island*.

8 f Norman Taurog's *Living It Up* was a remake of William Wellman's *Nothing Sacred*.

9 h Tim Whelan's *Step Lively* was a remake of the Marx Brothers' *Room Service*.

10 a Dick Powell's *You Can't Run Away From It* was a remake of Frank Capra's *It Happened One Night*.

■ **139.** Both answers are correct. In some prints, "Mother of God" was changed to "Mother of mercy" in order to avoid any possible objection by the United Council of Churches.

■ **140.** D. W. Griffith.

■ **141.** Richard Boleslawski's *Rasputin and the Empress*.

■ **142.** **1 e** *The Human Interest Story* was the working title for Billy Wilder's *Ace in the Hole*.

2 h *Passport to Fame* was the working title for John Ford's *The Whole Town's Talking*.

3 c *An Affair of the Heart* was the working title for Robert Rossen's *Body and Soul*.

4 j *Dead Right* was the working title for Don Siegel's *Dirty Harry*.

5 d *Homicide* was the working title for Jules Dassin's *The Naked City*.

6 b *Miracle on 49th Street* was the working title

for Ben Hecht's and Charles MacArthur's
The Scoundrel.

7 a *Sleep No More* was the working title for Don
Siegel's *Invasion of the Body Snatchers.*

8 g *Golden Warriors* was the working title for
Elia Kazan's *On the Waterfront.*

9 f *Diamond in the Pavement* was the working
title for the Marx Brothers' *Love Happy.*

10 i *The Whip Master* was the working title for
Elia Kazan's *Baby Doll.*

143. *I'm a Stranger Here Myself.*

144. (c) Jean Renoir's *La Règle du Jeu* and (d) Sergei
Eisenstein's *Battleship Potemkin.*

145. Orson Welles's *Citizen Kane.* In 1952, Vittorio De
Sica's *Bicycle Thief* finished first.

146. Stanley Donen's and Gene Kelly's *Singin' in the
Rain,* which finished fourth in 1982.

147. Stanley Kubrick's *2001: A Space Odyssey.*

148. (c) John Ford's *The Searchers,* (e) Alfred Hitchcock's *Vertigo,* and (f) Stanley Donen's and Gene
Kelly's *Singin' in the Rain.*

149. Ingmar Bergman's *Wild Strawberries* and *Persona.*

150. None of them. From top to bottom, the 1992 list:
Orson Welles, Jean Renoir, Jean-Luc Godard,
Alfred Hitchcock, Charlie Chaplin, John Ford,
Satyajit Ray, Yasujiro Ozu, Carl Theodor Dreyer,
and Sergei Eisenstein.

151. *They Shoot Horses, Don't They?* (novel by Horace
McCoy; directed by Sidney Pollack).

152. *The Wild Child* (François Truffaut).

153. *Deliverance* (novel by James Dickey; directed by
John Boorman).

154. *The King of Comedy* (Martin Scorsese).

155. *Porcile (Pig Pen)* (Pier Paolo Pasolini).

- **156.** *Darling* (John Schlesinger; script by Frederic Raphael).
- **157.** *Husbands* (John Cassavetes).
- **158.** *Lola Montès* (Max Ophuls).
- **159.** *Once Upon a Time in the West* (Sergio Leone)
- **160.** *Stromboli* (Roberto Rossellini).

QUIZ THREE

The Answers

■ **161.** This one is tricky, so give yourself partial credit if your answer was child-actor Roddy McDowall in John Ford's *How Green Was My Valley*. Actually, the film is narrated by the McDowall character after he's become an adult, and Irving Pichel, a director himself, delivered the narration, though he is never seen on screen.

■ **162.** Malcolm McDowell in Stanley Kubrick's production of Anthony Burgess's *A Clockwork Orange*.

■ **163.** Title introducing Akira Kurosawa's *Seven Samurai*.

■ **164.** Jimmy Cagney in Billy Wilder's *One, Two, Three*.

■ **165.** Michael Redgrave in L. P. Hartley's *The Go Between*, directed by Joseph Losey.

■ **166.** Lea Massari in Michelangelo Antonioni's *L'avventura*.

■ **167.** False. Sam Fuller served in the First Infantry Division during World War II and wrote a war novel called *The Big Red One*, from which he made his 1980 film. All of the information about Budd Boetticher is incorrect. Don Siegel's *Hell Is for Heroes* has nothing to do with *The Big Red One*

168. 1 Josef von Sternberg   c *Fun in a Chinese Laundry*
      2 *Lillian Hellman*   d *Scoundrel Time*
      3 *King Vidor*   a *A Tree Is a Tree*
      4 *Ben Hecht*   f *A Child of the Century*
      5 *Errol Flynn*   b *My Wicked, Wicked Way*
      6 *Mae West*   e *Goodness Had Nothing to
                                 Do With It*

169. UFA (Universum Film Aktien Gesellschaft)

170. Marlon Brando and Robert De Niro, who both played Vito Corleone. Brando won an Oscar for Best Actor in Francis Coppola's *The Godfather* De Niro won an Oscar for Best Supporting Actor in Coppola's *The Godfather, Part II*

171. All played Joan of Arc. Renée Falconetti in Carl Theodor Dreyer's *The Passion of Joan of Arc*, Jean Seberg in Otto Preminger's *Saint Joan*, Florence Delay in Robert Bresson's *The Trial of Joan of Arc*, Ingrid Bergman in Roberto Rossellini's *Joan of Arc at the Stake* and Victor Fleming's *Joan of Arc*.

172. Each was its leading man's last film: Humphrey Bogart in *The Harder They Fall*, Spencer Tracy in *Guess Who's Coming to Dinner*, Montgomery Clift in *The Defector*, Gary Cooper in *The Naked Edge*, John Wayne in *The Shootist*.

173. Before they turned to directing, all were cameramen or cinematographers.

174. All take place during the Civil War.

175. All feature exciting car chases.

176. Alfred Hitchcock's *Vertigo*, in which Tom Helmore gets away with murdering his rich wife.

177. Neorealism.

178. 1 a François Truffaut's *Stolen Kisses* was dedicated to the French Cinémathèque and Henri Langlois.

2 d Jacques Demy's *Lola* was dedicated to Max Ophuls.

3 b François Truffaut's *The Wild Child* was dedicated to Jean-Pierre Léaud.

4 e Jean Luc-Godard's *Made in U.S.A.* was dedicated to Nick [Ray] and Samuel [Fuller], whose pupil I am in terms of sight and sound.

5 f William Wellman's *Roxie Hart* was dedicated to all the beautiful women in the world who shot their men full of holes out of pique.

6 c Francis Coppola's *The Outsiders* was dedicated to the people who first suggested that it be made—librarian Jo Ellen Misakian and the students of Lone Star School in Fresno, California.

■ **179.** (e) Akira Kurosawa's *The Hidden Fortress*.

■ **180.** (b) Akira Kurosawa's *Yojimbo*.

■ **181.** Gloria Swanson to a group of reporters, photographers, and newsreel men in Billy Wilder's *Sunset Boulevard*.

■ **182.** Oskar Werner, after the cremation of Jeanne Moreau and Henri Serre, in François Truffaut's *Jules and Jim*.

■ **183.** Gig Young in Sydney Pollack's production of Horace McCoy's *They Shoot Horses, Don't They?*

■ **184.** Joseph Cotten to Agnes Moorehead about Dolores Costello and Tim Holt in Orson Welles's production of Booth Tarkington's *The Magnificent Ambersons*.

■ **185.** Peter Sellers, as a mad ex-Nazi scientist, to Peter Sellers, as the President of the United States, in Stanley Kubrick's *Dr. Strangelove or: How I Learned to Stop Worrying and Love the Bomb* .

QUIZ THREE

⭐ ⭐

The Answers

186. Marlon Brando in Laslo Benedek's *The Wild One.*

187. Title introducing Jean Cocteau's *La Belle et la bête* (*Beauty and the Beast*).

188. Jeanne Moreau, in a voice-over, to either Oskar Werner or Henri Serre (or both of them) in François Truffaut's *Jules and Jim.*

189. Danielle Darrieux, selling her famous earrings to a jeweler, in Max Ophuls's *The Earrings of Madame de . . . .*

190. Joel McCrea to Robert Warwick and Porter Hall in Preston Sturges's *Sullivan's Travels.*

191. (c) Dick Powell's *The Conqueror.* Among the dead, in addition to John Wayne: Powell, Susan Hayward, Pedro Armendariz, Agnes Moorehead, and Thomas Gomez.

192. Thelma Ritter, who had memorable moments in Joseph L. Mankiewicz's *All About Eve,* Sam Fuller's *Pickup on South Street,* Alfred Hitchcock's *Rear Window,* Frank Capra's *A Hole in the Head,* and John Huston's *The Misfits.*

■ **193.** **1** Edward Dmytryk   **d** *It's a Hell of a Life But Not a Bad Living*
   2 Jean Renoir   **b** *My Life and My Films*
   3 Frank Capra   **e** *The Name Above the Title*
   4 Budd Schulberg   **f** *Moving Pictures*
   5 Charlie Chaplin   **a** *My Life in Pictures*
   6 Vincente Minnelli   **c** *I Remember It Well*

■ **194.** (b) *Persona.*

■ **195.** Maida Vale is the London telephone exchange—i.e., the *M* in Alfred Hitchcock's *Dial M for Murder.*

■ **196.** Fathers directing their daughters: Jenny Hecht in Ben's *Actors and Sin*, Barbara Hawks in Howard's *The Big Sky*, Anjelica Huston in John's *A Walk With Love and Death*, Patricia Hitchcock in Alfred's *Strangers on a Train*, Liza Minnelli in Vincente's *A Matter of Time.*

■ **197.** Each was the director's first feature in color.

■ **198.** Famous directors directing famous directors. Roman Polanski directed John Huston in *Chinatown*. Jean-Luc Godard directed Fritz Lang in *Contempt*. Milos Forman directed Nicholas Ray in *Hair*. Jean-Luc Godard directed Sam Fuller in *Pierrot le fou*. Charlie Chaplin directed Buster Keaton in *Limelight*. Max Ophuls directed Vittorio De Sica in *The Earrings of Madame de . . . . .*

■ **199.** All feature titles designed by Saul Bass.

■ **200.** All were X-rated when first released.

■ **201.** True.

■ **202.** (d) Howard Hawks's *Scarface.*

■ **203.** **1 d** Sam Fuller's *The Steel Helmet* was dedicated to the United States Infantry.
   2 a Jean-Luc Godard's *Breathless* was dedicated to Monogram Pictures.
   3 c John Ford's *3 Godfathers* was dedicated to the memory of Harry Carey—bright star

of the Western sky.

4 e Ridley Scott's *Blade Runner* was dedicated to Philip K. Dick.

5 b Preston Sturges's *Sullivan's Travels* was dedicated to the memory of those who made us laugh: the motley mountebanks, the clowns, the buffoons, in all times and in all nations, whose efforts have lightened our burden a little.

■ **204.** Rin Tin Tin, a German shepherd found in a German trench during World War I. Warner Brothers was the studio.

■ **205.**

1	Curzio Malaparte	**e**	*Strange Deception*
2	Thomas McGuane	**d**	*92° in the Shade*
3	Norman Mailer	**g**	*Maidstone*
4	Ben Hecht	**j**	*Specter of the Rose*
5	George Axelrod	**f**	*Lord Love a Duck*
6	Ernest Lehman	**a**	*Portnoy's Complaint*
7	Clifford Odets	**h**	*Nothing But the Lonely Heart*
8	Susan Sontag	**c**	*Duet for Cannibals*
9	Marguerite Duras	**b**	*Days in the Trees*
10	Abraham Polonsky	**i**	*Force of Evil*

■ **206.** Edmond O'Brien to Robert Ryan in Sam Peckinpah's *The Wild Bunch*.

■ **207.** Anthony Perkins, who has crossed over into the personality of his mother, in Alfred Hitchcock's *Psycho*.

■ **208.** Giancarlo Giannini in Lina Wertmuller's *Swept Away*.

■ **209.** Chorus of small boys in Carl Theodor Dreyer's *Vampyr*.

■ **210.** Superimposed over the face of Louis Malle's *Lacombe, Luçien*.

Quiz Three

★ ★ ★

The Answers

■ **211.** René Auberjonois in Robert Altman's *Brewster Mc-Cloud*.

■ **212.** Tadeusz Lomniki in Andrej Wajda's *A Generation* (Part One of the Wajda Trilogy).

■ **213.** Alain Delon in Jean-Pierre Melville's *Dirty Money*.

■ **214.** John Garfield in Abraham Polonsky's *Force of Evil*.

■ **215.** Martin Scorsese, in a voice-over, in his *Mean Streets*.

■ **216.** **1 c** Donald Ogden Stewart used the pseudonym Gilbert Holland for Philip Leacock's *Escapade*.

2 e Dalton Trumbo used the pseudonym Robert Rich for Irving Rapper's *The Brave One*.

3 g Ben Hecht used the pseudonym Lester Bartow for Otto Preminger's *Whirlpool*.

4 d Ring Lardner Jr. used the pseudonym Philip Rush for Pat Jackson's *Virgin Island*.

5 a Hugo Butler used the pseudonym H. B. Addis for Luis Buñuel's *The Young One*.

6 h Lester Cole used the pseudonym Gerald L. C. Copley for James Hill's *Born Free*.

7 f Carl Foreman used the pseudonym Derek
Frye for Joseph Losey's *The Sleeping Tiger*.

8 b Howard Koch used the pseudonym Peter
Howard for Joseph Losey's *A Finger of
Guilt/The Intimate Stranger*.

217. Georges Franju.

218.
1 Frances Marion	**d**	*Off With Their Heads*
2 Mervyn LeRoy	**e**	*Take One*
3 Philip Dunne	**f**	*Take Two*
4 Lester Cole	**b**	*Hollywood Red*
5 Jesse Lasky Jr.	**c**	*Whatever Happened to Hollywood?*
6 Raoul Walsh	**a**	*Each Man in His Time*

219. Marlon Brando.

220. Silvio Narizzano's *Die! Die! My Darling!*, which
starred Tallulah Bankhead, Stefanie Powers, and
Donald Sutherland.

221. In each, a woman falls to her death: Magda
Schneider in *Liebelei*, Kim Novak in *Vertigo*, Kath-
leen Byron in *Black Narcissus*, Brigitte Bardot in *A
Very Private Affair*, Nicole Berger in *Shoot the Piano
Player*, Dominique Sanda in *Une Femme douce*.

222. All feature Sam Peckinpah as an actor.

223. Each has a noted writer—or writers—in the cast:
Norman Mailer in *Ragtime*, James Leo Herlihy in
Four Friends, James Dickey in *Deliverance*, Ben
Hecht and Charles MacArthur in *Crime Without
Passion*, Jerzy Kosinski in *Reds*.

224. They all include at least one sequence in color.

225. All end with the sound of laughter.

226. Lionel, Alfred, and Randy Newman.

227. Gloria Grahame was the actress, Nicholas Ray the
director, and Anthony Ray the director's son.

228. **1 b** Martin Scorsese's *Raging Bull* is dedicated
to Haig P. Manoogian.

2 d Wim Wenders's *Wings of Desire* is dedicated to all the former angels but especially to Yasujiro [Ozu], François [Truffaut], and Andrej [Wajda].

3 a Martin Scorsese's *The King of Comedy* is dedicated to Dan Johnson.

4 c Wim Wenders's *Summer in the City* is dedicated to The Kinks.

229. True.

230. (c) They refused to see films featuring men in uniform.

231. Virginia Huston to Dickie Moore about Robert Mitchum and Jane Greer in Jacques Tourneur's *Out of the Past*.

232. Jean-Marie Patte, as King Louis XIV, quoting a maxim of La Rochefoucauld's in Roberto Rossellini's *La Prise de pouvoir par Louis XIV*.

233. Orson Welles about Rita Hayworth in his *The Lady From Shanghai*.

234. Producer Roger Corman bought an awful Russian science-fiction movie, *Planet of Storms*, and turned it over to Peter Bogdanovich, who, when ordered to "stick some girls in," cast Mamie Van Doren and a bevy of blonde starlets, rewrote the story, shot new footage, supervised the dubbing, and then tied the whole thing together with his own offscreen narration. The last lines are an obvious homage to the last lines of Orson Welles's *The Lady From Shanghai* Though credited to "Derek Thomas," *Voyage to the Planet of Prehistoric Women* can be considered Bogdanovich's first film as a director. "I made it as *Gill-Women of Venus*. You see how art is corrupted."

235. Harrison Ford about Sean Young in Ridley Scott's *Blade Runner*

QUIZ FOUR

The Answers

236. Wesley Addy to Ralph Meeker in Robert Aldrich's production of Mickey Spillane's *Kiss Me Deadly*.

237. Walter Brennan to Gary Cooper in Frank Capra's *Meet John Doe*.

238. Marlene Dietrich to Gary Cooper in Josef von Sternberg's *Morocco*.

239. Clifton Webb to Dana Andrews about Gene Tierney in Otto Preminger's *Laura*.

240. Anthony Quinn to Peter O'Toole in David Lean's *Lawrence of Arabia*.

241. False.

242. (b) Jean Renoir's *Toni*, a forerunner of neorealism.

243. Jimmy Cagney, who smacked Mae Clarke in the face with a grapefruit in William Wellman's *The Public Enemy* (in real life, a hood named Earl "Hymie" Weiss did the deed), sat in his mother's lap in Raoul Walsh's *White Heat*, and played a top cop in Milos Forman's *Ragtime*.

244. Walter Hill's *The Long Riders*, in which David, Keith, and Robert Carradine played Cole, Jim, and Bob Younger; James and Stacy Keach played Jesse and Frank James; Dennis and Randy Quaid played Ed and Clell Miller; Nicholas and Christopher Guest played Bob and Charlie Ford

245. Kenneth Anger's *Scorpio Rising.*

246. Richard Lester's *A Hard Day's Night.*

247. Howard Hawks's *Only Angels Have Wings.*

248. Federico Fellini's *8½*

249. George Cukor's production of Clare Booth's play, *The Women*

250. George Stevens's *Shane*

251. True.

252. ZaSu Pitts.

253.

1 *The Moon and Sixpence*	**c** Paul Gauguin
2 *All the King's Men*	**d** Huey Long
3 *Raging Bull*	**h** Jake La Motta
4 *Citizen Kane*	**g** William Randolph Hearst
5 *The Miracle Worker*	**f** Helen Keller
6 *Reds*	**b** John Reed
7 *Yankee Doodle Dandy*	**a** George M. Cohan
8 *Beloved Infidel*	**e** F. Scott Fitzgerald

254. Burt Lancaster.

255. John Huston (Best Director, Best Screenplay) and his father Walter (Best Supporting Actor), for *The Treasure of the Sierra Madre.*

256. *Nanook of the North* (Robert Flaherty).

257. *Limelight* (Charlie Chaplin).

258. *Two English Girls* (François Truffaut).

259. *The Treasure of the Sierre Madre* (novel by B. Traven; directed by John Huston).

260. *Land of the Pharaohs* (Howard Hawks).

261. *The Blackboard Jungle* (Richard Brooks).

262. *The French Connection* (William Friedkin).

263. *GoodFellas* (Martin Scorsese).

264. *Bram Stoker's Dracula* (Francis Coppola).

265. *Henry: Portrait of a Serial Killer* (John McNaughton).

Quiz Four
★ ★

The Answers

266. Peter Lorre to a jury of criminals in Fritz Lang's *M*.
267. Claudia Cardinale to Jason Robards about Charles Bronson in Sergio Leone's *Once Upon a Time in the West*.
268. Confession written out by Thorkild Roose for Anne Svierkier to sign, in Carl Theodor Dreyer's *Vredens Dag* (*Day of Wrath*).
269. John Wayne in Don Siegel's *The Shootist*.
270. Kathleen Turner to William Hurt in Lawrence Kasdan's *Body Heat*.
271. Otto Preminger's *Anatomy of a Murder*.
272. A clip from Erich von Stroheim's *Queen Kelly* was shown in Billy Wilder's *Sunset Boulevard*, in which both Swanson and Stroheim appeared.
273.
1 Irving Thalberg	d MGM
2 Carl Laemmle	i Universal
3 David O. Selznick	e RKO
4 Harry Cohn	g Columbia
5 B. P. Schulberg	h Paramount

　　6 Darryl F. Zanuck　　**b** 20th Century-Fox
　　7 Samuel Z. Arkoff　　**c** American-International
　　8 D. W. Griffith　　　**j** United Artists
　　9 James Carreras　　　**a** Hammer
　　10 Mike Todd　　　　　**f** Magna

■ **274.** True.

■ **275.** George Cukor's *Les Girls.*

■ **276.** Jean Renoir's *La Règle du jeu.*

■ **277.** Martin Scorsese's *Mean Streets.*

■ **278.** Max Ophuls's *Lola Montès.*

■ **279.** F. W. Murnau's *Nosferatu* and F. W. Murnau's and Robert Flaherty's *Tabu.*

■ **280.** Yasujiro Ozu's *An Autumn Afternoon.*

■ **281.**　**1 e** Brigitte Bardot reads *Fritz Lang* in Jean-Luc Godard's *Contempt.*

　　2 g Jayne Mansfield reads Grace Metalious's *Peyton Place* in Frank Tashlin's *Will Success Spoil Rock Hunter.*

　　3 a Oskar Werner reads Charles Dickens's *David Copperfield* in François Truffaut's *Fahrenheit 451.*

　　4 h Sean Connery reads *Sexual Adventures of the Criminal Female* in Alfred Hitchcock's *Marnie.*

　　5 f Ronald Colman reads William Shakespeare's *Othello* in George Cukor's *A Double Life.*

　　6 c Ernst Deutsch reads Holly Martins's *Oklahoma* in Carol Reed's *The Third Man.*

　　7 d Jean Seberg reads William Faulkner's *The Wild Palms* in Jean-Luc Godard's *Breathless* and Valerie Kaprisky reads it in Jim McBride's eponymous remake.

　　8 b Several actors and actresses read *Ancient Weird Religious Rites* in Herschell Gordon Lewis's *Blood Feast.*

282. Rudolph Maté's *D.O.A.*, which starred Edmond O'Brien.

283.
1	*Star!*	e	Gertrude Lawrence
2	*Beau James*	f	Jimmy Walker
3	*Song Without End*	g	Franz Liszt
4	*Deep in My Heart*	c	Sigmund Romberg
5	*I'll Cry Tomorrow*	a	Lillian Roth
6	*Gentleman Jim*	b	Jim Corbett
7	*Man of a Thousand Faces*	d	Lon Chaney
8	*Cell 2455, Death Row*	h	Caryl Chessman

284. John Huston's production of Stephen Crane's *The Red Badge of Courage*, which also starred Audie Murphy, World War II's most decorated GI.

285. True.

286. *High Heels* (Pedro Almodovar).

287. *Reservoir Dogs* (Quentin Tarantino).

288. *Body Heat* (Lawrence Kasdan).

289. *The Killer* (John Woo).

290. *Death in Venice* (Luchino Visconti; novel by Thomas Mann).

291. *Bad Lieutenant* (Abel Ferrara).

292. *Divorce Italian Style* (Pietro Germi).

293. *I Married a Witch* (René Clair).

294. *Out of the Past* (Jacques Tourneur).

295. *Baby Doll* (Elia Kazan; screenplay by Tennessee Williams).

Quiz Four

The Answers

■ **296.** Robert Giraud in Jean Marboeuf's *Vaudeville.*
■ **297.** Dennis Hopper to Bruno Ganz in Wim Wender's *The American Friend.*
■ **298.** Peggy Cummins to John Dall in Joseph H. Lewis's *Gun Crazy.*
■ **299.** Jack Palance to Burt Lancaster in Richard Brooks's *The Professionals.*
■ **300.** Barbara Stanwyck to Robert Ryan in Fritz Lang's *Clash by Night.*
■ **301.** Harry Houdini.
■ **302.**

1	Charlie Chaplin	**c**	Roland Totheroh
2	Buster Keaton	**a**	Elgin Lessley
3	Carol Reed	**i**	Robert Krasker
4	D. W. Griffith	**f**	Billy Bitzer
5	Clint Eastwood	**b**	Bruce Surtees
6	Budd Boetticher	**e**	Lucien Ballard
7	Erich von Stroheim	**h**	William Daniels
8	Douglas Sirk	**d**	Russell Metty
9	Robert Aldrich	**g**	Joseph Biroc

■ **303.** True. It was based on Vidal's *The Death of Billy the Kid.*

■ **304.**   **1 c**   William Holden was the original choice for the Farley Granger role in Alfred Hitchcock's *Strangers on a Train.*

2 h   Noel Coward was the original choice for the Orson Welles role in Carol Reed's *The Third Man.*

3 e   Clifton Webb was the original choice for the Claude Rains role in Alfred Hitchcock's *Notorious.*

4 g   Grace Kelly was the original choice for the Eva Marie Saint role in Elia Kazan's *On the Waterfront.*

5 j   Cary Grant was the original choice for the Jimmy Stewart role in Alfred Hitchcock's *Rope.*

6 a   John Garfield was the original choice for the Dick Powell role in Edward Dmytryk's *Murder, My Sweet.*

7 b   Ronald Colman was the original choice for the Gregory Peck role in Alfred Hitchcock's *The Paradine Case.*

8 d   George Raft was the original choice for the Humphrey Bogart role in Dashiell Hammett's *The Maltese Falcon*, directed by John Huston.

9 k   Vera Miles was the original choice for the Kim Novak role in Alfred Hitchcock's *Vertigo.*

10 l   Paul Newman was the original choice for the Clint Eastwood role in Don Siegel's *Dirty Harry.*

11 i   Burt Lancaster was the original choice for the Joseph Cotten role in Alfred Hitchcock's *Under Capricorn.*

12 f Gary Cooper was the original choice for the Joel McCrea role in *Alfred Hitchcock's* Foreign Correspondent.

■ **305.** (d) Raimu, the French actor who starred in Marcel Pagnol's *César* and Julian Duvivier's *Un Carnet de bal.*

■ **306.** *Paisan,* Roberto Rossellini.

■ **307.** *Heaven Can Wait,* Ernst Lubitsch.

■ **308.** *The Naked Dawn,* Edgar G. Ulmer.

■ **309.** *Jules and Jim,* François Truffaut.

■ **310.** *Casablanca,* Michael Curtiz.

■ **311.** **1 d** Dorothy Malone reads Willa Cather's *My Antonia* in Douglas Sirk's *The Tarnished Angels.*

2 b Richard Harris reads Irving Shulman's *Cry Tough* in Lindsay Anderson's *This Sporting Life* (novel by David Storey).

3 f Eddie Constantine reads Raymond Chandler's *The Big Sleep* in Jean-Luc Godard's *Alphaville.*

4 i Jean-Pierre Léaud reads *Japanese Women* in François Truffaut's *Bed and Board.*

5 a Harvey Keitel reads F. Scott Fitzgerald's *Tender Is the Night* in Martin Scorsese's *Who's That Knocking at My Door.*

6 c Dominique Sanda reads William Shakespeare's *Hamlet* in Robert Bresson's *Une Femme douce.*

7 h James Coburn reads Mikhael Bakunin's *The Patriotism* in Sergio Leone's *Duck, You Sucker!*

8 j David Niven reads Alexander Alekhine's *My Best Games of Chess* in Michael Powell's and Emeric Pressburger's *Stairway to Heaven/A Matter of Life and Death.*

9 g Charles Aznavour reads *La Timidité* in
François Truffaut's *Shoot the Piano Player.*
10 e Jennifer Jones reads *Spells and Charms of
Mary Woodus* in Michael Powell's and
Emeric Pressburger's *the Wild Heart.*

312. Ingmar Bergman and Orson Welles.

313.
1	*The Great Moment*	**c**	William T. G. Morton
2	*Gaily, Gaily*	**h**	Ben Hecht
3	*Too Much, Too Soon*	**f**	Diana Barrymore
4	*The Long Gray Line*	**b**	Martin Maher
5	*Birdman of Alcatraz*	**g**	Robert Stroud
6	*The Magic Box*	**a**	William Friese-Greene
7	*The Wrong Man*	**e**	Marry Balestrero
8	*The Wings of Eagles*	**d**	Frank "Spig" Wead

314. True. Clint Eastwood starred with Silvano
Mangano in Vittorio De Sica's segment of *The
Witches* (1966).

315. King Vidor. Picture unknown.

316. *Taxi Driver* (Martin Scorsese).

317. *Underworld* (Josef von Sternberg; script by Ben
Hecht).

318. *I Confess* (Alfred Hitchcock).

319. *Shane* (George Stevens).

320. *The Barefoot Contessa* (Joseph L. Mankiewicz).

321. *White* (Krzysztof Kieslowski).

322. *The Pornographer* (Shohei Imamura).

323. *The Milky Way* (Luis Buñuel).

324. *Spetters* (Paul Verhoeven).

325. *Applause* (Rouben Mamoulian).

326. *The Passenger* (Michelangelo Antonioni).

327. *The Grapes of Wrath* (John Ford; novel by John
Steinbeck).

328. *Dawn of the Dead* (George Romero).

329. *The Black Cat* (Edgar G. Ulmer).

330. *Band of Angels* (Raoul Walsh).

The Answers

- **331.** Title introducing Luchino Visconti's *Senso*, superimposed over Act III of *Il Trovatore*, "Di quella pira... "
- **332.** Joseph Cotten in Carol Reed's *The Third Man*.
- **333.** Nathalie Baye about Charles Denner in François Truffant's *The Man Who Loved Women*.
- **334.** Anton Walbrook in Max Ophuls's *La Ronde*.
- **335.** Humphrey Bogart about Ava Gardner in Joseph L. Mankiewicz's *The Barefoot Contessa*.
- **336.** Norma (George Jessel's wife) and Constance Talmadge.
- **337.** *La nouvelle vague* (the New Wave).
- **338.** Irving Thalberg and Norma Shearer.
- **339.** William Faulkner.
- **340.** Sydney Pollack's *The Way We Were*.
- **341.** Sam Fuller, playing Sam Fuller, in Jean-Luc Godard's *Pierrot le fou*.
- **342.** Billy Wilder. Andrew Marton, a well-known second-unit director (with full-director credit for a number of fifties and sixties films), staged the ac-

tion scenes in William Wyler's *Ben-Hur*, Anthony Mann's *The Fall of the Roman Empire*, Nicholas Ray's *55 Days at Peking*, etc.

343. Ingmar Bergman.

344. Nicholas Ray.

345. Alfred Hitchcock.

346.

1 WHAT IS TRUTH		**c**	George Cukor's *Les Girls*
2 THEY CAN HAVE MY GUN WHEN THEY PRY IT FROM MY COLD DEAD FINGERS		**d**	John Milius's *Red Dawn*
3 THE WORLD IS YOURS		**f**	Howard Hawks's *Scarface* and Brian De Palma's *Scarface*
4 DEATH FROM ABOVE		**a**	Francis Coppola's *Apocalypse Now*
5 SAVE A SOUL MISSION		**b**	Joseph L. Mankiewicz's *Guys and Dolls*
6 BATES MOTEL		**e**	Alfred Hitchcock's *Psycho*

347. Federico Fellini's *La dolce vita*.

348. Graham Greene.

349. Joel McCrea, whose memorable 1962 Western was Sam Peckinpah's *Ride the High Country*.

350. In Alfred Hitchcock's *Stage Fright*, Richard Todd is guilty of murder, though the director allows us to believe otherwise for much of the picture.

351. Jameson Thomas to Sam Jaffe about Marlene Dietrich in Josef von Sternberg's *The Scarlet Empress*.

352. Daniel Day-Lewis to Robert Sean Leonard, in Martin Scorsese's production of Edith Wharton's *The Age of Innocence*.

353. Marlon Brando, in a voice-over, in Francis Coppola's *Apocalypse Now*.

■ **354.** Nathalie Baye about Charles Denner and the book he wrote about the women he loved in François Truffaut's *The Man Who Loved Women*

■ **355.** Marlene Dietrich in Josef von Sternberg's *The Blue Angel* (novel by Henrich Mann)

QUIZ FIVE ☆ ☆

The Answers

356. Ward Bond about John Wayne in John Ford's *The Quiet Man*.

357. Title introducing Jean Renoir's *The Golden Coach*.

358. A barker in Marcel Carné's *Les Enfants du paradis* (script by French poet Jacques Prévert).

359. Jack Lemmon in Billy Wilder's *The Apartment*.

360. Voice-over in Jean-Pierre Melville's *Bob le flambeur*

361. (a) Montgomery Clift and Elizabeth Taylor in George Stevens's *A Place in the Sun*.

362. Jean Vigo, whose *Zéro de conduite* was banned in France from the mid-thirties to the midforties.

363. **1 e** Jacques Tourneur's *Out of the Past* was based on Geoffrey Homes's *Build My Gallows High*.

  2 h John Brahm's *The Brasher Doubloon* was based on Raymond Chandler's *The High Window*

  3 n François Truffaut's *Shoot the Piano Player* was based on David Goodis's *Down There*.

  4 b John Boorman's *Point Blank* was based on Richard Stark's *The Hunter*.

5 i Allan Dwan's *Slightly Scarlet* was based on James M. Cain's *Love's Lovely Counterfeit.*

6 m Alfred Hitchcock's *Secret Agent* was based on W. Somerset Maugham's *Ashenden.*

7 a Orson Welles's *A Touch of Evil* was based on Whit Masterson's *Badge of Evil.*

8 l Alfred Hitchcock's *Vertigo* was based on Pierre Boileau's and Thomas Narcejac's *D'Entre les morts.*

9 k Robert Aldrich's *The Grissom Gang* was based on James Hadley Chase's *No Orchids for Miss Blandish.*

10 d Abraham Polonsky's *Force of Evil* was based on Ira Wolfert's *Tucker's People.*

11 o Alfred Hitchcock's *Spellbound* was based on Francis Beeding's *The House of Dr. Edwardes.*

12 c Paul Bogart's *Marlowe* was based on Raymond Chandler's *The Little Sister.*

13 j Alfred Hitchcock's *Suspicion* was based on Francis Iles's *Before the Fact.*

14 g Peter Yates's *Bullitt* was based on Robert L Pike's *Mute Witness.*

15 f Alfred Hitchcock's *Sabotage* was based on Joseph Conrad's *The Secret Agent.*

■ **364.** True. Chaplin's *Monsieur Verdoux*, based on an idea of Orson Welles's, told the story of a middle-aged man who met, married, and murdered women for their money.

■ **365.** Budd Boetticher's *Bullfighter and the Lady*, which starred Robert Stack, Gilbert Roland, Joy Page, and Katy Jurado.

■ **366.** John Cassavetes.

■ **367.** D. W. Griffith.

■ **368.** Sam Peckinpah.

■ **369.** Satyajit Ray, talking about *Aparajito*, Part Two of his Apu Trilogy.

■ **370.** Vittorio De Sica.

■ **371.**

1 HMS JONAH	**e**	Billy Wilder's *The Private Life of Sherlock Holmes*
2 MATUSCHEK & CO.	**c**	Ernst Lubitsch's *The Shop Around the Corner*
3 FIGHTERS FOR FULLER	**a**	Elia Kazan's *A Face in the Crowd*
4 HOSPITAL MANULANI	**f**	John Ford's *Donovan's Reef*
5 CHE SERA SERA	**b**	Joseph L. Mankiewicz's *The Barefoot Contessa*
6 STATION	**d**	Sergio Leone's *Once Upon a Time in the West*

■ **372.** (c) By order of Mussolini in 1935 to propagate the glory of the fascist regime.

■ **373.**

1 Tay Garnett	**a**	*A Man Laughs Back*
2 Richard Brooks	**l**	*The Brick Foxhole*
3 Erich von Stroheim	**k**	*Paprika*
4 Michael Powell	**f**	*A Waiting Game*
5 Edmund Goulding	**c**	*One for the Book*
6 Orson Welles	**d**	*Mr. Arkadin*
7 Jean Renoir	**i**	*The Notebooks of Captain Georges*
8 Sam Fuller	**j**	*Burn, Baby, Burn!*
9 Albert Lewin	**h**	*The Unaltered Cat*
10 Elia Kazan	**b**	*The Arrangement*
11 Pier Paolo Pasolini	**g**	*The Ragazzi*
12 Emeric Pressburger	**e**	*Killing a Mouse on Sunday*

■ **374.** *The Magnificent Ambersons*, Orson Welles. The staircase is pictured in number 418 of the Photo Quiz

■ **375.** Columbia Pictures' Harry Cohn.

■ **376.** Jean Seberg, in Jean-Luc Godard's *Breathless*, wondering what the dying Jean-Paul Belmondo has just called her.

■ **377.** Anonymous voices in Jean-Luc Godard's *Wind From the East*.

■ **378.** William Demarest about Barbara Stanwyck in Preston Sturges's *The Lady Eve*.

■ **379.** Joan Fontaine, in a voice-over, to Louis Jourdan in Max Ophuls's production of Stefan Zweig's *Letter From an Unknown Woman*.

■ **380.** Aldo Fabrizi's dying words in Roberto Rossellini's *Rome, Open City*.

QUIZ FIVE

⭐ ⭐ ⭐

The Answers

381. Riccardo Fellini in Federico Fellini's *I Vitelloni*.

382. Voice-over in Wim Wenders's *Wings of Desire*.

383. The leader of a scientific expedition, explaining what to feed a snake, to Henry Fonda in Preston Sturges's *The Lady Eve*.

384. The narrator in Budd Boetticher's *Bullfighter and the Lady*.

385. Voice-over in Roberto Rossellini's *Francesco, giullare di Dio* (*Francis, God's Jester*, usually mistitled *The Little Flowers of St. Francis*.)

386. Victor McLaglen.

387. (d) Less than forty.

388. **1 e** François Truffaut's *Mississippi Mermaid* was based on William Irish's *Waltz Into Darkness*.

   2 i Hobart Henley's *Roadhouse Nights* was based on Dashiell Hammett's *Red Harvest*.

   3 h Fritz Lang's *The Woman in the Window* was based on J. H. Wallis's *Once Off Guard*.

   4 g Jean-Luc Godard's *Band of Outsiders* was based on Dolores Hitchens's *Fool's Gold*.

5 c Stanley Kubrick's *The Killing* was based on Lionel White's *Clean Break.*

6 l Orson Welles's *The Lady From Shanghai* was based on Sherwood King's *Before I Die.*

7 m Claude Chabrol's *A Double Tour* (a.k.a. *Leda*) was based on Stanley Ellin's *The Key to Nicholas Street.*

8 f Alfred Hitchcock's *Frenzy* was based on Arthur LaBern's *Goodbye Piccadilly, Farewell Leicester Square.*

9 a Fritz Lang's *While the City Sleeps* was based on Charles Einstein's *The Bloody Spur.*

10 n Alfred Hitchcock's *The Lady Vanishes* was based on Ethel Lina White's *The Wheel Spins.*

11 k Joseph L. Mankiewicz's *House of Strangers* was based on Jerome Weidman's *I'll Never Go There Anymore.*

12 b Joseph H. Lewis's *My Name Is Julia Ross* was based on Anthony Gilbert's *The Woman in Red.*

13 j Alfred Hitchcock's *Family Plot* was based on Victor Canning's *The Rainbird Pattern.*

14 d Robert Siodmak's *Cry of the City* was based on Richard Murphy's *The Chair for Martin Rome.*

389. Stewart Granger.

390. Jean-Luc Godard chose (a) Max Ophuls's *Le Plaisir* as the greatest title and (f) Douglas Sirk's *A Time to Love and a Time to Die* as the runner-up.

391. Luis Buñuel.

392. Roberto Rossellini.

393. Carl Theodor Dreyer.

394. Edgar G. Ulmer.

395. Charlie Chaplin.

396. **1** THIS GIRL IS NOT   **f** Raoul Walsh's
           GUILTY WITH ME.   *Colorado Territory*
           WES MCQUEEN

        2 TO-NIGHT GOLDEN   **d** Alfred Hitchcock's
           CURLS   *The Lodger*

        3 HICKORY WOOD FARM **c** John Huston's *The
                                     Asphalt Jungle*

        4 JEREMIAH   **e** Jean-Luc Godard's
           PRODUCTIONS   *Contempt*

        5 ZELTON JEWELERS   **g** Nicholas Ray's *They
                                     Live by Night*

        6 BREAK O'DAWN CLUB   **a** Edgar G. Ulmer's *Detour*

        7 I AM HAPPY TO DRIVE **b** Frank Borzage's *Desire*
           A BRONSON **8**

397. True. Tati accepted but the film was never made.

398. *Under Capricorn*, which contains several long takes, most notably an incredibly fluid dinner-party sequence and the scene in which Ingrid Bergman confesses that she, not Joseph Cotten, is guilty of her brother's death.

399. Roberto Rossellini's *Rome, Open City*, the script for which was written by Rossellini, Sergio Amidei, and Federico Fellini.

400. Tyrone Power Sr. died during the filming of Norman Z. McLeod's *The Miracle Man*. Tyrone Power Jr. died during the filming of King Vidor's *Solomon and Sheba*.

401. Emil Hass Christensen to Birgitta Federspiel in Carl Theodor Dreyer's *Ordet*.

402. Karen Steele about Ray Danton in Budd Boetticher's *The Rise and Fall of Legs Diamond*.

403. The last title card in D. W. Griffith's *Intolerance*.

404. Voice-over, in Andrei Konchalovsky's *Runaway Train*, of two run-together lines from Shakespeare's *Richard III*, Act I, Scene 2—

ANNE: "Villain, thou know'st no law of God nor

man: no beast so fierce but knows some
touch of pity."

RICHARD: "But I know none, and therefore am no
beast."

◾ **405.** Maurice Ronet's last thoughts, superimposed over
his dead face, in Louis Malle's adaptation of Pierre
Drieu La Rochelle's *Le Feu follet* (*The Fire Within*).

PHOTO QUIZ

The Answers

406. *Intolerance* (D. W. Griffith, 1916).
407. *Greed* (Erich von Stroheim, 1924).
408. *Battleship Potemkin* (Sergei Eisenstein, 1925).
409. *The Gold Rush* (Charlie Chaplin, 1925).
■ **410.** *The General* (Buster Keaton and Clyde Bruckman, 1927).
411. *The Passion of Joan of Arc* (Carl Theodor Dreyer, 1928).
412. *City Lights* (Charlie Chaplin, 1930).
413. *Le Million* (René Clair, 1930).
414. *L'Atalante* (Jean Vigo, 1934).
415. *Le Jour se lève* (Marcel Carné, 1939).
416. *La Règle du jeu* (Jean Renoir, 1939).
417. *Citizen Kane* (Orson Welles, 1941).
418. *The Magnificent Ambersons* (Orson Welles, 1942).
419. *Brief Encounter* (David Lean, 1945).
420. *Ivan the Terrible* (Sergei Eisenstein, 1943–46).
421. *Louisiana Story* (Robert Flaherty, 1947).
422. *La terra trema* (Luchino Visconti, 1948).
423. *The Bicycle Thief* (Vittorio De Sica, 1949).

- **424.** *Singin' in the Rain* (Gene Kelly and Stanley Donen, 1952).
- **425.** *Tokyo Story* (Yasujiro Ozu, 1953).
- **426.** *Ugetsu Monogatari* (Kenji Mizoguchi, 1953).
- **427.** *Seven Samurai* (Akira Kurosawa, 1954).
- **428.** *Pather Panchali* (Satyajit Ray, 1955).
- **429.** *The Searchers* (John Ford, 1956).
- **430.** *Wild Strawberries* (Ingmar Bergman, 1957).
- **431.** *Vertigo* (Alfred Hitchcock, 1958).
- **432.** *L'avventura* (Michelangelo Antonioni, 1960).
- **433.** *8½* (Federico Fellini, 1963).
- **434.** *Persona* (Ingmar Bergman, 1967).
- **435.** *2001: A Space Odyssey* (Stanley Kubrick, 1968).

QUIZ SIX

The Answers

436. Warren Beatty, telling a farmer what he and Faye Dunaway do, in Arthur Penn's *Bonnie and Clyde*.

437. Deborah Kerr and Richard Burton in Tennessee Williams's *The Night of the Iguana*, directed by John Huston.

438. Edward G. Robinson to Richard Gaines in Billy Wilder's *Double Indemnity*.

439. Scott Wilson to Robert Blake in Richard Brooks's production of Truman Capote's *In Cold Blood*.

440. George M. Cohan's traditional thank-you speech (delivered, of course, by Jimmy Cagney) to Vaudeville and theater audiences (and, when he's given the Congressional Medal of Honor, to Captain Jack Young as President Franklin D. Roosevelt) in Michael Curtiz's *Yankee Doodle Dandy*.

441. Tallulah Bankhead in Alfred Hitchcock's *Lifeboat*.

442. John Ford's *Two Rode Together*, which starred Jimmy Stewart and Richard Widmark.

443. (c) D. W. Griffith.

444. (c) René Clair's *A nous la liberté*. Obviously, the suit was filed after the fall of France but before the United States entered the war.

445. *La politique des auteurs* (the *auteur* theory).

446. Marilyn Monroe.

447. Charlie Chaplin and Virginia Cherrill in Chaplin's *City Lights*.

448. Clark Gable.

449. Marlene Dietrich.

450. Jean-Paul Belmondo.

451. Sam Peckinpah's *The Wild Bunch*.

452. Mae Marsh.

453. Alfred Hitchcock's *Strangers on a Train*.

454.

1 David Lean		**d**	Maurice Jarre
2 Sergio Leone		**a**	Ennio Morricone
3 Alfred Hitchcock		**e**	Bernard Herrmann
4 Roberto Rossellini		**b**	Renzo Rossellini
5 Federico Fellini		**c**	Nina Rota

455. Neorealist films simply didn't make money.

456. *Singin' in the Rain* (Gene Kelly and Stanley Donen).

457. *Badlands* (Terrence Malick).

458. *2001: A Space Odyssey* (Stanley Kubrick).

459. *North by Northwest* (Alfred Hitchcock).

460. *Cabaret* (Bob Fosse).

461. *East of Eden* (Elia Kazan; novel by John Steinbeck).

462. *American Gigolo* (Paul Schrader).

463. *Sylvia Scarlett* (George Cukor).

464. *Midnight Cowboy* (John Schlesinger).

465. *Horse Feathers* (Norman Z. McLeod).

The Answers

- **466.** Al Pacino to Robert Duvall about Lee Strasberg in Francis Coppola's The Godfather, Part II.
- **467.** Harrison Ford about Rutger Hauer in Ridley Scott's *Blade Runner*.
- **468.** George Harrison to a TV technician about Ringo Starr in Richard Lester's *A Hard Day's Night*.
- **469.** Dirk Bogarde to Julie Christie in John Schlesinger's *Darling* (script by Frederic Raphael).
- **470.** Jean-Luc Godard, in a voice-over, about Claude Brasseur, Anna Karina, and Sami Frey in Godard's *Band of Outsiders*.
- **471.** In D. W. Griffith's *The Birth of a Nation*, Raoul Walsh played John Wilkes Booth, John Ford played a Ku Klux Klansman, and Erich von Stroheim was an extra.
- **472.** **1** John Frankenheimer's *Seconds* — **e** You're middle-aged, tired, fat, sick of it all . .

  2 Edgar G. Ulmer's *Detour* — **d** Looks like it cost $25. . .

3 Martin Ritt's
The Molly Maguires

f *The Informer* meets *Rules of the Game* in a coal mine . . .

4 Noel Black's
Pretty Poison

a Boy psycho meets teen queen for love . . .

5 Mike Hodges's
Get Carter

b Guns and gangsters. .

6 Franklin Schaffner s
The War Lord

c Their love was enough to give paganism a good name.. .

■ **473.** Milan Kundera's *The Unbearable Lightness of Being.*

■ **474.** **1 h** Thornton Wilder worked on Hitchcock's *Shadow of a Doubt.*

2 d Anthony Shaffer worked on Hitchcock's *Frenzy.*

3 g Brian Moore worked on Hitchcock's *Torn Curtain.*

4 c Dorothy Parker worked on Hitchcock's *Saboteur.*

5 j Ben Hecht worked on Hitchcock's *Notorious.*

6 i Ernest Lehman worked on Hitchcock's *North by Northwest*

7 b Arthur Laurents worked on Hitchcock's *Rope.*

8 f Raymond Chandler worked on Hitchcock's *Strangers on a Train*

9 e Maxwell Anderson worked on Hitchcock's *The Wrong Man.*

10 a James Hilton and Robert Benchley worked on Hitchcock's *Foreign Correspondent*

■ **475.** Mickey Rooney

■ **476.** James Dean

■ **477.** Katharine Hepburn

■ **478.** Jimmy Stewart.
■ **479.** Ingrid Bergman in Roberto Rossellini's *Stromboli, Voyage in Italy,* and *Europa '51*
■ **480.** Humphrey Bogart.
■ **481.** True.
■ **482.**   **1** Joseph H. Lewis's   **c** Now that everybody's
        The Big Combo   crazy for guns . . .
      2 Martin Ritt's *Edge*   **e** If you loved *On the*
        of the City   *Waterfront* . .
      3 Jacques Rivette's   **f** The *ultimate* film about
        Paris Belongs to Us   paranoia.
      4 Jack Webb's *Pete*   **g** The horn man shows
        Kelly's Blues   some *Gatsby* soul .
      5 Robert Wise's *The*   **a** Clenched-fists-in-
        Set-Up   leather *noir* . . .
      6 Michael Ritchie's   **b** Hot lead, cold sausages,
        Prime Cut   and orphanage flesh . . .
      7 Tony Richardson's   **d** The Big Guy's favorite
        The Entertainer   role . . . (the Big Guy
                being, of course,
                Laurence Olivier).

■ **483. a** Carl Foreman.
■ **484.**   **1 d** In John Ford's *7 Women,* Anne Bancroft says
        "So long, you bastard."
      2 e In Orson Welles's *Citizen Kane,* Welles says
        "Rosebud."
      3 f In Charlie Chaplin's *Monsieur Verdoux,*
        Chaplin says, "Ah, just a moment, I've
        never tasted rum."
      4 h In Stanley Kubrick's *2001: A Space Odyssey,*
        HAL sings, "Daisy, Daisy, give me your
        answer do. . . ."
      5 g In Otto Preminger's *Laura,* Clifton Webb
        says, "Goodbye, my love."
      6 b In Raoul Walsh's *The Strawberry Blonde,* Alan

Hale says, "Biff, it's very funny. My teeth don't hurt anymore."

7 a In Edmund Goulding's *Dark Victory*, Bette Davis says, "I don't want to be disturbed."

8 c In Don Siegel's *The Killers*, Lee Marvin says, "Lady, I don't have the time."

■ **485.** William Wellman's *Wings*

■ **486.** *Pretty Poison* (Noel Black).

■ **487.** *Thelma and Louise* (Ridley Scott).

■ **488.** *The James Dean Story* (George W. George and Robert Altman).

■ **489.** *The Big Chill* (Lawrence Kasdan).

■ **490** *A Letter to Three Wives* (Joseph L. Mankiewicz).

QUIZ SIX

★ ★ ☆

The Answers

491. Fritz Ellerkamp, Hitler's projectionist, in Hans-Jürgen Syberberg's *Hitler, A Film From Germany*. Ellerkamp was a character invented by Syberberg for the film.

492. John Gielgud in Alan Resnais's *Providence* (script by David Mercer).

493. Jack Palance, as a lordly movie producer, to Michel Piccoli, Fritz Lang, and George Moll in Jean-Luc Godard's *Contempt*.

494. Walter Matthau to Patricia Neal about Andy Griffith in Elia Kazan's *A Face in the Crowd*.

495. Jack Palance to Wendell Corey in Robert Aldrich's production of Clifford Odets's *The Big Knife*.

496. Orson Welles's *Citizen Kane*.

497. Cary Grant.

498.   **1 f** Dick Richards was the original choice to direct Sydney Pollack's *Tootsie*.

      2 i Jean-Luc Godard was the original choice to direct Joseph Losey's *Eva*.

      3 h Fritz Lang was the original choice to direct

Anthony Mann's *Winchester '73.*

4 d Peter Yates was the original choice to direct Francis Coppola's *The Godfather.*

5 a Sergei Eisenstein was the original choice to direct Josef von Sternberg's production of Theodore Dreiser's *An American Tragedy.*

6 g John Boorman was the original choice to direct Burt Reynolds's *Sharky's Machine.*

7 k François Truffaut was the original choice to direct Arthur Penn's *Bonnie and Clyde.*

8 c Rouben Mamoulian was the original choice to direct Otto Preminger's *Laura.*

9 l Sidney Lumet was the original choice to direct Brian De Palma's *Scarface.*

10 e Sam Peckinpah was the original choice to direct Norman Jewison's *The Cincinnati Kid.*

11 b Anthony Mann was the original choice to direct Stanley Kubrick's *Spartacus.*

12 j William Wyler was the original choice to direct John Ford's *How Green Was My Valley.*

■ **499.** (e) Slavko Vorkapich.

■ **500.** Poetess Joy Gresham met and later married C. S. Lewis, their story first told in *Shadowlands* directed for British television by Norman Stone; then told once again in Richard Attenborough's film of the same name.

■ **501.** John Gielgud.

■ **502.** Greta Garbo.

■ **503.** Montgomery Clift.

■ **504.** Robert Mitchum.

■ **505.** Rudolph Valentino.

■ **506.** Michael Powell, *Peeping Tom.*

■ **507.** Fritz Lang.

■ **508.** 1 Ingmar Bergman   **f** Sven Nykvist
           2 Jean-Luc Godard   **d** Raoul Coutard

3 Michelangelo   **e** Gianni Di Venanzo
   Antonioni
4 Alain Resnais   **b** Sacha Vierny
5 Luchino Visconti   **c** Giuseppe Rotunno
6 Luis Buñuel   **h** Gabriel Figueroa
7 Claude Chabrol   **i** Jean Rabier
8 Sergei Eisenstein **j** Edward Tissé
9 Max Ophuls   **a** Christian Matras
10 Georges Franju   **g** Marcel Fradetal

509. (e) Vittorio De Sica's *Shoeshine* in 1947.

510. Jean-Luc Godard's *First Name: Carmen*.

511. *Performance* (Donald Cammell and Nicolas Roeg).

512. *McCabe & Mrs. Miller* (Robert Altman).

513. *The Kid* (Charlie Chaplin).

514. *El Dorado* (Howard Hawks).

515. *It's a Wonderful Life* (Frank Capra).

516. *Trust* (Hal Hartley).

517. *The Lady From Shanghai* (Orson Welles).

518. *Charley Varrick* (Don Siegel).

519. *Touch of Evil* (Orson Welles).

520. *Passion* (Jean-Luc Godard).

Quiz Seven

The Answers

- **521.** Jack Nicholson in Bob Rafelson's *The King of Marvin Gardens*.
- **522.** Grace Kelly, ostensibly talking about a picnic-lunch chicken, to Cary Grant in Alfred Hitchcock's *To Catch a Thief*.
- **523.** John Beck and James Coburn about Kris Kristofferson in Sam Peckinpah's *Pat Garrett & Billy the Kid*.
- **524.** Faye Dunaway to Jack Nicholson about Belinda Palmer in Roman Polanski's *Chinatown*.
- **525.** William Hurt to Tom Berenger, Glenn Close, Jeff Goldblum, Kevin Kline, Mary Kay Place, JoBeth Williams, and Meg Tilly in Lawrence Kasdan's *The Big Chill*.
- **526.** Mark Robson's *Return to Paradise*.
- **527.** Satyajit Ray's *Pather Panchali*.
- **528.** Frank Capra's *It's a Wonderful Life*.
- **529.** Anthony Mann's *El Cid*.
- **530.** Robert Altman's *McCabe & Mrs. Miller*, which starred Warren Beatty and Julie Christie.

531. The Ranown series, named after actor Randolph Scott and producer Harry Joe Brown, who produced most of the seven Westerns. The series consists of Boetticher's *7 Men From Now*, *The Tall T.*, *Decision at Sundown*, *Buchanan Rides Alone*, *Ride Lonesome*, *Westbound*, and *Commanche Station*

532. Woody Allen

533. Laurel and Hardy.

534. RKO.

535. Linda Hunt, who won a Best Supporting Actress Oscar for Peter Weir's *The Year of Living Dangerously*.

536. Josef von Sternberg, or Joe Stern as Robert Mitchum referred to him.

537. Leo McCarey. The two movies referred to are *Ruggles of Red Gap* and *The Awful Truth*.

538. Alfred Hitchcock.

539. Vincente Minnelli.

540. Fritz Lang.

541. *Kiss Me Deadly* (Robert Aldrich; novel by Mickey Spillane).

542. *Sweet Smell of Success* (Alexander Mackendrick).

543. *The Wrong Man* (Alfred Hitchcock).

544. *Natural Born Killers* (Oliver Stone).

545. *Lady in the Lake* (novel by Raymond Chandler; directed by Robert Montgomery). Because the movie was shot mainly from a subjective, first-person point of view, most of the action is seen by "You and Robert Montgomery."

QUIZ SEVEN

☆ ☆

The Answers

- **546.** Gene Hackman to a druggie in William Friedkin's *The French Connection*.
- **547.** Paul Muni to Osgood Perkins before firing a machine gun in Howard Hawks's *Scarface* (script by Ben Hecht).
- **548.** Girl sunbathing on the roof of a Roman high-rise, to other sunbathers, as a helicopter dangling a huge statue of Christ passes overhead, in Federico Fellini's *La dolce vita*.
- **549.** Jean Harlow to Jimmy Cagney in William Wellman's *The Public Enemy*.
- **550.** Peter Lorre in John Huston's *Beat the Devil* (script by Truman Capote).
- **551.** Stanley Kubrick on his *Dr. Strangelove or: How I Stopped Worrying and Learned to Love the Bomb*.
- **552.** Louis Malle's *The Fire Within* (based on Pierre Drieu La Rochelle's *Le Feu follet*), which starred Maurice Ronet.
- **553.** James Whale's *Bride of Frankenstein*.

■ **554.** Leo McCarey's *Make Way for Tomorrow*, the great American film about old age.

■ **555.** Howard Hawks's *Land of the Pharaohs*.

■ **556.**

1 Ben Hecht's *Specter of the Rose*
d The love story of a mad ballet dancer and a ballerina. . . .

2 Joseph Losey's *These Are the Damned*
f Teddy-boy rebels, a sci-fi cave under the rocks by the sea . . .

3 Don Levy's *Herostratus*
g A young poet turned cynical by society decides to kill himself. . . .

4 Ronald Neame's *Tunes of Glory*
b It's your regiment until some upper-class toff replaces you . . .

5 Albert Lewin's *Pandora and the Flying Dutchman*
a He was hundreds of years old and lived under a curse. . . .

6 Roy Ward Baker's *Five Million Years to Earth*
c You've seen it on TV and loved it. But you can't remember the title. . . .

7 Peter Watkins's *Edvard Munch*
e Bleak Norwegian skies. Religious repression. . .

■ **557.** Louis Lumière.

■ **558.**

1 g Lee Marvin was the original choice for the James Coburn role in Sam Peckinpah's *Major Dundee*.

2 b Marlon Brando was the original choice for the Edmund Purdom role in Michael Curtiz's *The Egyptian*.

3 d William Powell was the original choice for the Melvyn Douglas role in Ernst Lubitsch's *Ninotchka*.

4 h Richard Burton was the original choice for

the Albert Finney role in Malcolm Lowry's *Under the Volcano,* directed by John Huston.

5 e Grace Kelly was the original choice for the Elizabeth Taylor role in Tennessee Williams's *Cat on a Hot Tin Roof,* directed by Richard Brooks.

6 i Edward G. Robinson was the original choice for the Humphrey Bogart role in Archie Mayo's *The Petrified Forest.*

7 c Al Pacino was the original choice for the Richard Gere role in Francis Coppola's *The Cotton Club.*

8 j Elizabeth Taylor was the original choice for the Shirley MacLaine role in Don Siegel's *Two Mules for Sister Sara.*

9 f Montgomery Clift was the original choice for the Gary Cooper role in Fred Zinnemann's *High Noon.*

10 a Moira Shearer was the original choice for the Cyd Charisse role in Vincente Minnelli's *Brigadoon.*

■ **559.** (c) Frank Borzage's *History Is Made at Night.*

■ **560.**

1 Gillo Pontecorvo's *Burn!*	**d** A British agent teaches tropical blacks how to stage a revolution. . . .
2 John Flynn's *The Outfit*	**a** That *Walking Tall* guy and Col. Kilgore spray vengeful lead . . . (That *Walking Tall* guy is Joe Don Baker and Col. Kilgore is Robert Duvall.)
3 Peter Bogdanovich's *Saint Jack*	**e** The whorehouse *Great Gatsby* of Southeast Asia.

4 Michael Reeves's
   *Conqueror Worm/The
   Witchfinder General*

f A truly first-rate
   Vincent Price horror
   movie? Not really a
   horror movie
   though . . .

5 Roger Corman's
   Tomb of Ligeia

b A truly first-rate
   Vincent Price horror
   movie? Best of this
   series. . . .

6 Robert Aldrich's
   Ulzana's Raid

c A Vietnam fable or a
   film *really* about
   fighting the savages,
   whoever they are. . . .
   (The Big B is Burt
   Lancaster.)

561. Jacques Tati.

562. John Huston.

563. Anthony Mann.

564. Sergei Eisenstein.

565. Jacques Tourneur. The three films referred to are *Out of the Past, Canyon Passage,* and *I Walked With a Zombie.*

566. *Kiss of Death* (Henry Hathaway).

567. *Stalag 17* (Billy Wilder).

568. *Dial M for Murder* (Alfred Hitchcock).

569. *Tess* (novel by Thomas Hardy; directed by Roman Polanski).

570. *The Natural* (novel by Bernard Malamud; directed by Barry Levinson).

QUIZ SEVEN
☆ ☆ ☆

The Answers

571. Isa Miranda and Gérard Philipe in Max Ophuls's *La Ronde*.

572. A patient in an insane asylum in Sam Fuller's *Shock Corridor*

573. Rudy Vallee to Claudette Colbert about Joel McCrea in Preston Sturges's *The Palm Beach Story*.

574. Margit Carstensen in Rainer Werner Fassbinder's *The Bitter Tears of Petra von Kant*.

575. Marlene Dietrich to Mort Mills about Orson Welles in Welles's *Touch of Evil*.

576. Hans-Jürgen Syberberg.

577. Jean Cocteau

578. Wim Wenders.

579. Michelangelo Antonioni.

580. John Cassavetes.

581. (e) F. W. Murnau's *Sunrise*.

582. (c) Jimmy Stewart in Anthony Mann's *Bend of the River*.

583. 1 i *From Amongst the Dead* was the working title for Alfred Hitchcock's *Vertigo*.

2 g *The Gent From Frisco* was the working title for John Huston's *The Maltese Falcon.*

3 e *Smiler With a Gun* was the working title for John Farrow's *His Kind of Woman.*

4 c *Now It Can Be Told* was the working title for Henry Hathaway's *The House on 92nd Street.*

5 f *Behind This Mask* was the working title for Nicholas Ray's *In a Lonely Place.*

6 a *The Dark Tower* was the working title for Arthur Penn's *Night Moves.*

7 k *Mad with Much Heart* was the working title for Nicholas Ray's *On Dangerous Ground.*

8 d *Breathless* was the working title for Alfred Hitchcock's *North by Northwest.*

9 l *Your Red Wagon* was the working title for Nicholas Ray's *They Live by Night.*

10 b *News Is Made at Night* was the working title for Fritz Lang's *While the City Sleeps.*

11 j *Outbreak* was the working title for Elia Kazan's *Panic in the Streets.*

12 h *Night Cry* was the working title for Otto Preminger's *Where the Sidewalk Ends.*

■ **584.** 1944. Leo McCarey's *Going My Way* won Best Picture. The previous year, Michael Curtiz's *Casablanca* had to beat out nine other movies for the Oscar.

■ **585.** Alfred Hitchcock.

■ **586.** Nicholas Ray.

■ **587.** Michelangelo Antonioni.

■ **588.** François Truffaut.

■ **589.** Frank Capra.

■ **590.** Arthur Penn.

■ **591.** *Rope* (Alfred Hitchcock).

■ **592.** *Park Row* (Sam Fuller).

■ **593.** *Heaven's Gate* (Michael Cimino).

- **594.** *Don't Look Now* (Nicolas Roeg).
- **595.** *The Maltese Falcon* (novel by Dashiell Hammett; directed by John Huston).
- **596.** *Rio Bravo* (Howard Hawks).
- **597.** *Ride the High Country* (Sam Peckinpah).
- **598.** *Bullitt* (Peter Yates).
- **599.** *The Big Parade* (King Vidor).
- **600.** *Killer's Kiss* (Stanley Kubrick).

Quiz Eight

The Answers

■ **601.** Peter Boyle in John G. Avildsen's *Joe*.

602. Title introducing Sergei Eisenstein's *Ivan the Terrible, Part One*.

603. John Derek's credo in Nicholas Ray's *Knock on Any Door*.

604. Orson Welles to Joseph Cotten in Carol Reed's *The Third Man*.

605. Carleton Young to Jimmy Stewart about John Wayne in John Ford's *Rashomon*-like *The Man Who Shot Liberty Valance*.

■ **606.** Carole Lombard and Fredric March in William Wellman's *Nothing Sacred*.

607. A pregnant Ingrid Bergman considering suicide by throwing herself into an active volcano in Robert Rossellini's *Stromboli*.

608. Robert Mitchum in Charles Laughton's *The Night of the Hunter*.

609. Buster Keaton.

610. Brigitte Bardot.

611. Orson Welles.

- **612.** Jane Russell.
- **613.** John Wayne in Howard Hawks's *Rio Bravo*.
- **614.** Samuel Goldwyn.
- **615.** Wim Wenders's *The American Friend*. Directors in the cast include Nicholas Ray, Dennis Hopper, Gérard Blain, Jean Eustache, Sam Fuller, Peter Lilienthal, Daniel Schmid, and Sandy Whitelaw.
- **616.** Tippi Hedren, whose first two films were Alfred Hitchcock's *The Birds* and *Marnie*. Charlie Chaplin's *A Countess From Hong Kong* was her third. Melanie Griffith is her daughter.
- **617.** Tod Browning, *Freaks*.
- **618.** Robert Mitchum.
- **619.** *The Palm Beach Story* (Preston Sturges).
- **620.** *Johnny Guitar* (Nicholas Ray).
- **621.** *The Warriors* (Walter Hill).
- **622.** *The Third Man* (Carol Reed). The "he" is Anton Karas, who composed the famous musical score and played it entirely on a zither.
- **623.** *Easy Rider* (Dennis Hopper).
- **624.** *Who's Afraid of Virginia Woolf?* (play by Edward Albee; directed by Mike Nichols).
- **625.** *Naked Lunch* (novel by William S. Burroughs; directed by David Cronenberg).
- **626.** *Klute* (Alan J. Pakula).
- **627.** *A Clockwork Orange* (novel by Anthony Burgess; directed by Stanley Kubrick).
- **628.** *Dr. Strangelove or: How I Learned to Stop Worrying and Love the Bomb* (Stanley Kubrick).
- **629.** *Excalibur* (John Boorman).
- **630.** *The Old Man and the Sea* (novel by Ernest Hemingway; directed by John Sturges).

QUIZ EIGHT

☆ ☆

The Answers

631. Warren Beatty about Julie Christie in Robert Altman's *McCabe & Mrs. Miller*.

632. George C. Scott to Karl Malden about an ancient ruin in Franklin Schaffner's *Patton* (script by Francis Coppola).

■ **633.** Ernest Borgnine and William Holden about Robert Ryan in Sam Peckinpah's *The Wild Bunch*.

634. Henry Fonda in William Wellman's *The Ox-Bow Incident*.

635. Edgar Kennedy to Rex Harrison in Preston Sturges's *Unfaithfully Yours*.

636. F. Scott Fitzgerald, who coscripted Frank Borzage's *Three Comrades* and Jack Conway's *A Yank at Oxford* (uncredited).

637. Frank S. Nugent, who scripted John Ford's *Fort Apache*, *The Quiet Man*, and *The Searchers*.

638. Herman J. Mankiewicz, who scripted Orson Welles's *Citizen Kane* and coscripted George Cukor's *Dinner at Eight*.

■ **639.** Eleanor Perry, who scripted her husband Frank's *David and Lisa*, *The Swimmer*, and *Diary of a Mad Housewife*.

■ **640.** Donald Ogden Stewart, who scripted George Cukor's *The Philadelphia Story* and *Keeper of the Flame*.

■ **641.** Preston Sturges.

■ **642.** True.

■ **643.**
1 William Fraker's *Monte Walsh*
a Real—or, at least, almost real—cowboys from the author of *Shane* . . .

2 Preston Sturges's *Unfaithfully Yours* (the original version, not Howard Zieff's remake with Dudley Moore)
d Soaring romance, sweeping poetry . . .

3 Michael Powell's and Emeric Pressburger's *I Know Where I'm Going!*
b *Local Hero*-ine meets *The Quiet Man*. . . .

4 Robert Mulligan's *The Stalking Moon*
c *The Searchers* starring Freddy. . . .

■ **644.** False, though the tale has been told around Hollywood and in innumerable books for many years. Although Stroheim felt that wearing the undergarments would make his extras feel more "aristocratic," when B. P. Schulberg got wind of it, he canceled the order as an unnecessary expenditure.

■ **645.**
1 i Montgomery Clift was the original choice for the Paul Newman role in Walter Tevis's *The Hustler*, directed by Robert Rossen

2 f Deanna Durbin was the original choice for the Judy Garland role in Victor Fleming's *The Wizard of Oz*.

3 j Jane Fonda was the original choice for the Faye Dunaway role in Roman Polanski's *Chinatown*.

4 g Isabelle Adjani was the original choice for the Maruschka Detmers role in Jean-Luc Godard's *First Name: Carmen*.

5 h Gene Hackman was the original choice for the Robert Duvall role in Francis Coppola's *Apocalypse Now!*

6 d Lana Turner was the original choice for the Linda Darnell role in Otto Preminger's *Forever Amber*.

7 l John Derek was the original choice for the Montgomery Clift role in James Jones's *From Here to Eternity*, directed by Fred Zinnemann.

8 c Spencer Tracy was the original choice for the Edward G. Robinson role in Norman Jewison's *The Cincinnati Kid*.

9 a Kirk Douglas was the original choice for the Rock Hudson role in John Frankenheimer's *Seconds*.

10 b Elizabeth Taylor was the original choice for the Shirley MacLaine role in Billy Wilder's *Irma La Douce*.

11 k Joan Crawford was the original choice for the Deborah Kerr role in James Jones's *From Here to Eternity*, directed by Fred Zinnemann.

12 e Claudette Colbert was the original choice for the Bette Davis role in Joseph L. Mankiewicz's *All About Eve*.

■ **646.** True.

■ **647.**

1 Sam Fuller's *Park Row*

e Crusading little newspaper vs. the big combo. . . .

2 Larry Yust's *Homebodies*

g You're old, getting evicted, and live in Cincinnati. . . .

3 Robert Aldrich's *The Legend of Lylah Clair*

a Pygmalion plus model show up in Hollywood. . . .

4 Richard Sarafian's *Vanishing Point*

f Being chased, chasing the horizon, chasing himself, he speeds his Charger. . . .

5 Hubert Cornfield's *The Night of the Following Day*

b Aging lion-as-kidnapper only wants the money. . . .

6 Max Ophuls's *La signora di tutti*

d Naïf meets older man— Is it love? . . .

7 Carol Reed's *Outcast of the Islands*

c Up the river with Eisenstein: the Montage of Attractions meets. . . .

■ **648.** Luis Buñuel.

■ **649.** *Morocco* (Josef von Sternberg).

■ **650.** *The Women* (George Cukor; play by Clare Booth).

■ **651.** *Bitter Moon* (Roman Polanski).

■ **652.** *Wuthering Heights* (Luis Buñuel; novel by Emily Brontë).

■ **653.** "10" (Blake Edward).

■ **654.** *The Nutty Professor* (Jerry Lewis).

■ **655.** *The Yakuza* (Sydney Pollack).

QUIZ EIGHT
☆ ☆ ☆

The Answers

656. Tom Neal in Edgar G. Ulmer's *Detour.*

■ **657.** The Alpha 60 computer in Jean-Luc Godard's *Alphaville.*

■ **658.** Bruno S. in Werner Herzog's *The Mystery of Kaspar Hauser/Every Man for Himself and God Against All.*

659. Richard Dreyfuss to Steve Kanaly about Warren Oates in John Milius's *Dillinger.*

660. Rita Hayworth to Robert Scott in Charles Vidor's *Gilda.*

661. Silvana Mangano in Giuseppe De Santis's *Bitter Rice.*

662. Nina Pens Rode in Carl Theodor Dreyer's *Gertrude.*

663. Jessica Lange, reminiscing about the house in which she grew up in Sydney Pollack's *Tootsie.*

664. Gene Fowler, who scripted Richard Thorpe's *The Earl of Chicago* and coscripted George Cukor's *What Price Hollywood?* (uncredited).

■ **665.** Philip Dunne, who scripted Joseph L. Mankiewicz's *The Ghost and Mrs. Muir*, coscripted Otto Preminger's *Forever Amber*, and directed *Ten North Frederick*.

■ **666.** S. J. Perelman, who scripted Norman Z. McLeod's Marx Brothers movies *Monkey Business* and *Horse Feathers*, commenting on the socialist-realist fervor of Hollywood writers and intellectuals during the thirties.

■ **667.** Lester Cole—one of the Hollywood Ten—who coscripted Raoul Walsh's *Objective Burma* and André de Toth's *None Shall Escape*.

■ **668.** Howard Koch, who scripted Max Ophuls's *Letter From an Unknown Woman* and coscripted Michael Curtiz's *Casablanca*

■ **669.** (b) George Stevens's *A Place in the Sun*.

■ **670.** Vittorio De Sica's *Umberto D.*

■ **671.** Robert Burks didn't photograph Alfred Hitchcock's *Psycho* (1960) because the director wanted to make an extremely low-budget horror thriller and decided to use the technical crew from his television show, *Alfred Hitchcock Presents*. By shooting almost as cheaply as his B-picture imitators (William Castle, for example), Hitchcock could—and did—beat them at their own game. John L. Russell photographed *Psycho*.

■ **672.** (b) Lina Wertmuller for *Seven Beauties* (1976).

■ **673.** **1 b** In Otto Preminger's *Whirlpool*, José Ferrer says, "I'm afraid you're right, tonight I was a bit stupid."

　　　 2 d In John Sturges's *The Great Escape*, Donald Pleasance says, "Thank you for getting me out."

　　　 3 f In Nicholas Ray's *The Lusty Men*, Robert Mitchum says, "Guys like me last forever."

  4 e In Budd Boetticher's *The Rise and Fall of Legs Diamond*, Ray Danton says, "You can't kill me."

  5 a In Richard Brooks's *The Professionals*, Marie Gomez says, "Give us a kiss."

  6 c In Stanley Kubrick's *The Killing*, Marie Windsor says, "It's a bad joke without a punch line."

■ **674.** Jean Renoir's *La Nuit du carrefour*.

■ **675.** **1 c** Stuart Heisler's *I Died a Thousand Times* was a remake of Raoul Walsh's *High Sierra*.

  2 i Robert Sparr's *Once You Kiss a Stranger* was a remake of Alfred Hitchcock's *Strangers on a Train*.

  3 b Gordon Douglas's *The Fiend Who Walked the West* was a remake of Henry Hathaway's *Kiss of Death*.

  4 h Eddie Davis's *Color Me Dead* was a remake of Rudolph Maté's *D.O.A.*

  5 a Don Siegel's *The Hanged Man* was a remake of Robert Montgomery's *Ride the Pink Horse*

  6 e Robert D. Webb's *The Capetown Affair* was a remake of Sam Fuller's *Pickup on South Street*.

  7 k Harry Keller's *Step Down to Terror* was a remake of Alfred Hitchcock's *Shadow of a Doubt*.

  8 j William Dieterle's *Satan Met a Lady* was a remake of Roy Del Ruth's *The Maltese Falcon* (1931).

  9 l Taylor Hackford's *Against All Odds* was a remake of Jacques Tourneur's *Out of the Past*.

 10 f George Armitage's *Hit Man* was a remake ot Mike Hodges's *Get Carter*.

11 g Robert Alan Aurthur's *The Lost Man* was a remake of Carol Reed's *Odd Man Out*

12 d Louis Malle's *Crackers* was a remake of Mario Monicelli's *Big Deal on Madonna Street.*

676. Rex Harrison, ostensibly talking about conducting an orchestra, to Linda Darnell in Preston Sturges's *Unfaithfully Yours.*

677. (a) Italy.

■ **678.** Alfred L. Werker's *He Walked by Night*, in which Richard Basehart slogs through the sewers of Los Angeles. Anthony Mann directed much of the movie without receiving credit.

679. Jean-Luc Godard.

680. Frank Capra.

681. Jean Renoir.

682. Vittorio De Sica.

683. Anthony Mann.

■ **684.** Lee Garmes, who shot Howard Hawks's *Scarface*, Josef von Sternberg's *Morocco*, Victor Fleming's *Gone With the Wind*, and Edmund Goulding's *Nightmare Alley.* ·

685. Arthur Miller, who shot John Ford's *How Green Was My Valley*, William Wellman's *The Ox-Bow Incident*, Otto Preminger's *Whirlpool*, and Joseph Losey's *The Prowler.*

686. Stanley Cortez—not remembered for his color cinematography—who shot such black and white beauties as Orson Welles's *The Magnificent Ambersons*, Fritz Lang's *Secret Beyond the Door*, Charles Laughton's *The Night of the Hunter*, and Sam Fuller's *Shock Corridor.*

687. James Wong Howe, who shot William K. Howard's *The Power and the Glory*, Victor Sjöström's *Under the Red Robe*, Michael Curtiz's *Yankee Doodle Dandy*, and Robert Rossen's *Body and Soul.*

■ **688.** Leon Shamroy, who shot Fritz Lang's *You Only Live Once*, Elia Kazan's *A Tree Grows in Brooklyn*, and Joseph L. Mankiewicz's *Cleopatra*.

■ **689.** *Isn't Life Wonderful* (D. W. Griffith).

690. *These Are the Damned* (Joseph Losey).

691. *Viridiana* (Luis Buñuel).

— **692.** *The Night of the Iguana* (play by Tennessee Williams; directed by John Huston).

693. *The Great Train Robbery* (Edwin S. Porter).

694. *Splendor in the Grass* (Elia Kazan).

695. *The Assassination of Trotsky* (Joseph Losey).

696. *The Day the Earth Stood Still* (Robert Wise).

697. *Scarface* (Howard Hawks).

698. *8½* (Federico Fellini).

■ **699.** *Rocco and His Brothers* (Luchino Visconti).

■ **700.** *Once Upon a Time in America* (Sergio Leone).

701. *The Invasion of the Body Snatchers* (Don Siegel).